Now What?
Confronting Uncomfortable
Truths About Inequity in Schools

Dedications

Carmella S. Franco:

I dedicate this book to my husband, Tom, who has stood with me through the tremendous time demands of all that transpired during the past decade. He was very supportive of the second book and knows that the career aspirations of the new cadre of leaders are dependent on those who have gone before. I also remember my late mother, who was there for me throughout my career and to whom I am eternally grateful.

Maria G. Ott:

This book is dedicated to my eight grandchildren: Clare, Ella, Moira, Miranda, Lucia, Julian, Joseph, and Annalise. Thank you for always asking intriguing questions and offering amazing insights about life and the world. You are sunlight and laughter and make me hopeful for the future.

Darline P. Robles:

This book is dedicated to three women: to my mother, Mary Ocampo Parra, and my grandmother Refugio Ocampo—who taught me the importance of family through their actions, courage, and unconditional love—and to my daughter, Lauren, who inspires me every day and gives me hope for the future. Through Lauren, I know our family legacy will live on—Adelante, Lauren!

Now What?
Confronting Uncomfortable Truths About Inequity in Schools

A Leadership Rubric for Action

Carmella S. Franco

Maria G. Ott

Darline P. Robles

Foreword by Delores B. Lindsey
and Randall B. Lindsey

FOR INFORMATION:

Corwin

A SAGE Company

2455 Teller Road

Thousand Oaks, California 91320

(800) 233-9936

www.corwin.com

SAGE Publications Ltd.

1 Oliver's Yard

55 City Road

London EC1Y 1SP

United Kingdom

SAGE Publications India Pvt. Ltd.

B 1/I 1 Mohan Cooperative Industrial Area

Mathura Road, New Delhi 110 044

India

SAGE Publications Asia-Pacific Pte. Ltd.

18 Cross Street #10-10/11/12

China Square Central

Singapore 048423

President: Mike Soules

Vice President and
  Editorial Director: Monica Eckman

Program Director and Publisher: Dan Alpert

Senior Content Development
  Editor: Lucas Schleicher

Content Development Editor: Mia Rodriguez

Editorial Intern: Ricardo Ramirez

Production Editor: Tori Mirsadjadi

Copy Editor: Megan Speer-Levi

Typesetter: C&M Digitals (P) Ltd.

Cover Designer: Rose Storey

Marketing Managers:
  Olivia Bartlett and Melissa Duclos

Printed in Canada

Library of Congress Cataloging-in-Publication Data

Names: Franco, Carmella S., author. | Ott, Maria G., author. | Robles, Darline P., author.

Title: Now what? confronting uncomfortable truths about inequity in schools: a leadership rubric for action / Carmella S. Franco, Maria G. Ott, Darline P. Robles.

Description: Thousand Oaks, California : Corwin, [2023] | Includes bibliographical references and index.

Identifiers: LCCN 2022026712 | ISBN 9781071850763 (paperback) | ISBN 9781071850749 (epub) | ISBN 9781071850732 (epub) | ISBN 9781071850725 (pdf)

Subjects: LCSH: School management and organization—Social aspects—United States. | Educational equalization—United States. | Educational leadership—United States. | Multicultural education—United States. | Academic achievement—United States.

Classification: LCC LB2805 .F667 2023 | DDC 371.2/07—dc23 LC record available at https://lccn.loc.gov/2022026712

This book is printed on acid-free paper.

22 23 24 25 26 10 9 8 7 6 5 4 3 2 1

CONTENTS

FOREWORD
Three Voices. One Message.

A decade ago, three Latina superintendents who served urban school districts in California published their first book, *A Culturally Proficient Society Begins in School: Leadership for Equity*. In those ten years, these three superintendents continued honing their craft by continuing their "hands-on work" in school districts that have been historically overlooked. Drs. Franco, Ott, and Robles continue their "hands-on" work in our schools and, just as important, make their presence known in state and national professional leadership organizations. As you will see when reading this important work, the authors hold as deep beliefs that all students have the capacity to learn and achieve at high levels and that our schools have the capacity to educate all children and youth to high levels. We are honored to have had the distinct pleasure to know and work with these remarkable leaders for more than twenty years.

Franco, Ott, and Robles characterized their first book as timely and relevant as they shared their experiences in moving schools and school districts to address individual and systemic inequities that fostered low engagement with communities and unacceptably low achievement of students. They are consistent in identifying leadership actions necessary to overcome barriers to student achievement and parent engagement.

Today, the authors frame the message in this book as urgent. They note that too many students and communities were left behind during the pandemic, which created an immediate shift to learning in virtual formats. *Now What? Confronting Uncomfortable Truths About Inequity in Schools* is a call to action. Using the Culturally Proficient Framework, the authors present case stories as successful models for implementation. The authors expertly provide a step-by-step template for leaders to use in designing and implementing actions intended to narrow access and achievement gaps for historically marginalized students in schools.

This book is written by leaders for leaders who are ready to act no matter how uncomfortable their current reality might be. The risks of inaction for our students are much too high to seek comfort in today's complex educational environment. The desired state for educational leaders must engage community, political, religious, law enforcement, mental health, and educational leaders in shared decision-making to overcome barriers for equitable schools, in both virtual and face-to-face experiences. No longer can we wait for the next crisis or the next best practice or the next expert to face our uncomfortable truths about inequities in schools. The field of education has experienced equity mandates and manipulations for well over fifty years. The time is now. Let's join these authors on this well-charted journey toward success for all learners.

Delores B. Lindsey, Retired Professor,
California State University San Marcos

Randall B. Lindsey, Emeritus Professor,
California State University, Los Angeles

Co-Founders, Center for Culturally Proficient Educational Practice

ACKNOWLEDGMENTS

We are most appreciative of those who have supported and encouraged us in the writing of this new book. As such, it is important to thank and recognize those who have played a meaningful role in our lives, in particular during this past decade.

Carmella S. Franco

I have experienced a time of amazing professional achievements while also experiencing losses. That has been the story for many others also, and it is important that I include it here. In the first book, *A Culturally Proficient Society Begins in School: Leadership for Equity,* I included a brief excerpt about a dear couple, Nellie and David, community members who were there for me when I began my first principal position and who were supportive of all that I did in my educational consultant work. Sadly, Nellie and David were victims of COVID-19, and their loss is significant for me. I also lost my beloved mother, Margaret, a profound void in my life now, and my dear Aunt Marie, who I wrote about in the first book. This decade saw the passing of kind, supportive longtime friends Rocco Crupi and Joan Gazdik.

Even in a time of challenge and change in one's personal life, one must move forward. Thankfully, one individual and a solid rock for me, husband Tom Jackson, was a consistent beacon of encouragement in whatever door opened for me, and many doors opened during the past ten years. I acknowledge my dear friends and fellow authors, Maria and Darline, for wanting to join together as a trio in leaving the legacy of a second book. I am extremely grateful to Stephanie Graham, who was a tremendous resource and support during the writing of our book. I also want to acknowledge my family and friends for rallying behind me as I embarked on each new, exciting professional experience. I have found a niche in working with school boards and superintendents, both of whom have faced such incredible challenges with grace. It is gratifying to see the renewed commitment to vision and mission, all for the benefit of students. After all, it is not about adults; it is about the students, the future leaders of our country. I love my work and approach it with enthusiasm and anticipation of positive results, and I want to continue making a difference in everything I do. In my eyes, this book is a symbol of hope for leaders who are trying to move their districts toward Cultural Proficiency and equity, and I am proud to be on this journey with them as an author.

Maria G. Ott

The journey to share what we know now that we didn't know then was possible because three very different women who share a common passion for diversity, equity, and inclusion came together in collaboration and willingness to learn and grow. Our respected colleague Stephanie Graham-Rivas was at our side during many difficult conversations to help us arrive at how we would tell the story behind this book. Special thanks to Carmella and Darline for joining me in this endeavor. We are like a Venn diagram where three distinct circles intersect, and it is in this intersection that our book resides.

I also thank my husband, Tom Ott, who had a difficult year due to health issues. Tenacious in fighting for recovery, he showed me that pain is part of life. When it seemed that this book would have to be put on hold, he encouraged me to push forward with my co-authors.

I have special appreciation for being part of an extraordinary university that encourages faculty to contribute to scholarly work. Former dean Karen Gallagher was an inspiration to me as she led the University of Southern California Rossier School of Education for twenty years and never lost her ability to innovate and challenge our thinking about how to promote equity and opportunity for all students. Dean Pedro Noguera arrived in 2019 and brought a sense of urgency to Rossier as he stepped in during a global pandemic. He is showing the way to be breakthrough educators and leaders. Inspiration and courage surround me at USC Rossier, and I know that I am fortunate to be part of a faculty team committed to social justice and preparing the next generation of change leaders.

Darline P. Robles

Since March 16, 2020, I have counted my blessings in knowing so many individuals who have been part of my family, friends, and colleagues throughout my career. I am forever grateful for your love and friendship. Special thanks and gratitude go to my family. To my husband, Frank, who has been by my side for over fifty years, guiding, supporting, and encouraging me to continue to fight for social justice. To my mother, who continues to provide our family with all the love and strength to inspire all of us to do better and be kind to others. To my brother Lorenzo, who since childhood has been with me cheering me on. To my son, Lawrence, who provided examples from his own life about the inequities young Brown men face every day and how we must fight the injustices for all Brown and Black men. To my daughter, Lauren, who is a true gift in my life. I thank God every day for sending her to me as an example of what the future can be—an equity warrior who shows up every day, ready to take on the world for those less privileged than her. Lauren, you inspire me every day to do better. To those I have worked with in the past and work with today, thank you for your willingness to help me grow and be part of your lives. I can only do what I do because I have each of you in my life, and for that I will be forever grateful. I hope this book provides you with the guidance you need to act to make the educational system work for children who have not been served well by the system. If not you or me, then who?

We three authors are grateful beyond words to Stephanie Graham for her assistance with and caring guidance of our work. In our first book, she played a major role in the construction of the Cultural Proficiency Leadership Rubric. It was a joy to have Stephanie revisit with us the use of the rubric as a key signature piece of the journey to equitable practices.

PUBLISHER'S ACKNOWLEDGMENTS

Corwin gratefully acknowledges the contributions of the following reviewers:

Jeff Austin
Principal
Social Justice Humanitas Academy
Los Angeles, CA

Shannon Hobbs-Beckley
Director of Teaching and Learning
Graded—American School of São Paulo
São Paulo, Brazil

Lena Marie Rockwood
Assistant Principal
Revere Public Schools
Revere, MA

Tanna H. Nicely
Executive Principal
South Knoxville Elementary
Knoxville, TN

ABOUT THE AUTHORS

Carmella S. Franco taught and began her administrative work in the Rowland Unified School District, served as a principal in grades K–8 in Bassett Unified School District, and headed the Personnel Department in the Lennox School District. Dr. Franco was selected as superintendent of the Whittier City School District in 1996, serving twelve years at the helm of that district before retiring in 2008. She began an interim superintendent position in the Woodland Joint Unified School District located outside of Sacramento the very next day. Dr. Franco served as interim superintendent for the Compton Unified School District, and prior to that assignment, she was appointed by the State Board of Education to serve as the state trustee for the Alisal Union School District. She presently is a search consultant for Hazard Young Attea & Associates in California, helping school boards with their superintendent searches, and at the state level, Dr. Franco served for fourteen years as one of the directors of the Association of California School Administrators (ACSA) Superintendents Academy.

Dr. Franco's personal motto "Making a difference in everything I do" has not changed since she entered the field of education and is still relevant now as she is a consultant with a specialty in governance. Throughout her career, Dr. Franco has worked for the good of her colleagues, often using her volunteer involvement in professional organizations, and has served as president of a number of them, including ACSA Region 14, California City School Superintendents, and the California Association of Latino Superintendents and Administrators. She was recognized as a founding member of the Association of Latino Administrators and Superintendents and received its Lifetime Achievement Award. Currently, she sits on the boards of the YMCA of Greater Whittier and the Rio Hondo College Foundation. Whether it is coordinating the recognition of local teachers or helping award scholarships to deserving community college students, Dr. Franco finds the work to be fulfilling and a commitment to the future.

Dr. Franco is an alumna of California State University at Los Angeles (CSULA), where she graduated cum laude with a degree in music and a master's degree in elementary education, and also earned two credentials. Her doctorate in nontraditional negotiation methods was received from the University of La Verne (ULV). She has lectured in the past at both CSULA and ULV in the area of educational administration and is a mentor in the USC Rossier Urban Superintendents' Academy. A book co-authored by Dr. Franco and her two colleagues Dr. Maria G. Ott and Dr. Darline P. Robles, titled *A Culturally Proficient Society Begins in School: Leadership for Equity*, was published in September 2011.

 *Maria G. Ott* holds the Irving R. and Virginia A. Melbo Chair in Education Administration at the USC Rossier School of Education. Dr. Ott served for more than forty years as an educator in K–12 urban school systems, including fourteen years as a superintendent and five years as senior deputy superintendent of the Los Angeles Unified School District. Her transition to higher education was an opportunity to apply her experiences to the preparation of leaders for school systems, colleges and universities, and other organizations.

Dr. Ott designed and launched the USC Rossier Urban Superintendents Academy in 2015 in partnership with AASA to prepare diverse and equity-minded leaders for K–12 school system leadership. She serves as a member of the Association of Latino Administrators and Superintendents (ALAS) Board of Directors to promote the goal of advancing diverse leaders who work to close opportunity and achievement gaps for Latino youth. She was honored with the 2021–2022 ALAS Lifetime Achievement Award and received the USC Rossier Dean's Superintendents Advisory Group (DSAG) Achievement Award in 2017. Dr. Ott is recognized for her leadership and advocacy for bilingual education and programs for English-language learners, leadership development for women, and public-private partnerships in education. She is a founding member of the California Association of Latino Superintendents and Administrators (CALSA) and ALAS.

Her work on Cultural Proficiency is detailed in her book, *A Culturally Proficient Society Begins in School: Leadership for Equity,* with co-authors Carmella S. Franco and Darline P. Robles. Dr. Ott has presented to national audiences on the topic of her book and continues to contribute to the educational literature about the importance of Cultural Proficiency in closing achievement gaps.

Darline P. Robles is the associate dean of the Office of Equity and Community Engagement and a professor of clinical education at the Rossier School of Education, University of Southern California. She teaches in the EdD educational leadership program and is the faculty adviser for the preliminary administrator credential under professional development. She also serves as a co-director of the Center on Education Policy, Equity and Governance. Dr. Robles serves as Rossier's diversity liaison to the University of Southern California diversity and inclusion efforts.

Prior to joining the faculty at Rossier, Dr. Robles served eight years as the first Latina county superintendent of the Los Angeles County Office of Education (LACOE), the nation's largest regional service agency. LACOE serves more than two million preschool and school-age children, of whom 60 percent are Latino. As chief of the Salt Lake City School District from 1995 to 2002, she was recognized for raising student achievement. Prior to her position in the Salt Lake City School District, she served as superintendent of the

Montebello Unified School District in California, where she began her teaching career. While superintendent, she saved the district from a state takeover. Her career has focused on serving underserved students and inspiring and mentoring young Latino educators.

Dr. Robles was named twice as one of *Hispanic Business* magazine's Top 100 Influential Hispanic Americans. In 2010 she was named to President Obama's Advisory Commission on Educational Excellence for Hispanics. Recent recognitions include the Education Medal from the Lucille and Edward R. Roybal Foundation in 2019 and the Mexican American Legal Defense and Educational Fund (MALDEF) Lifetime Achievement Award for Excellence in Community Service in 2022.

Dr. Robles is committed to public service and serves on many local and national boards. She presents to national audiences on leadership and Cultural Proficiency and is a leadership consultant to school districts and non-profit organizations.

CHAPTER 1

· ·

INTRODUCTION

"The goal is not to be better than the other man, but better than your previous self."

Dalai Lama XIV

Our first book was written to share our experiences as three Latina superintendents who led urban school districts and navigated the ladder to success during the lingering misogyny and racism of the twenty-first century. It was intended to motivate others to do the crucial work of moving organizations to address inequalities, attitudes, and behaviors that perpetuate inequalities. The book supported leaders in moving their systems forward by developing an awareness of the need for change and a commitment to Cultural Proficiency. The book was timely and relevant.

A lot has stayed the same, and so much has changed since 2011. At the ten-year anniversary of the book *A Culturally Proficient Society Begins in School: Leadership for Equity*, a second book is **urgent.** The national divide over important social, economic, and political issues has never been greater, and the threats to our democracy and Constitution have never been more real. Fractured government, threats to voter freedom, social upheaval, an ongoing and mutating pandemic, conspiracy theories, and lies and half-truths from government leaders—all fueled by ever-present partisan media sources, including unchecked social media—have brought this nation to important crossroads of crisis. No institution has been more affected than public education. As a microcosm of society, public education as we know it and its near-total collapse during the pandemic has hit families and communities hard. Schools and the public they serve had to rethink the entire teaching/learning enterprise, including the delivery of many public services to families.

The glaring inequity in schools pre-pandemic has been made worse, as too many students and families were further left behind by inadequate resources for online learning and a lack of other resources and support services that students and families most in need count on for their well-being and survival. While most students suffered educational lags during the pandemic, some students were affected more than others. As a result, some students have fallen woefully behind academically, have dropped out, are lacking credits to graduate or transfer to college, or have simply fallen off our radar screens. Even if schooling were to get back to pre-pandemic standards, too many students lost too much for too long for even the most compassionate and capable of us to help them catch up. We should not be surprised that the most vulnerable students during this time represent members of the same student demographic groups that have been, and who continue to be, the most underserved in our society. These are largely students of color, English learners, economically disadvantaged students, migrant students, and students with special needs. The access, opportunity, and achievement gaps most significant for these groups have grown deeper and will continue to widen unless compassionate and committed individuals conduct some form of concerted and calculated triage to prioritize treatment and intervention. The times call for educational and other public leaders to confront this challenge, take risks, and do whatever it takes to arrest the loss of progress for too many students who matter. As a microcosm of society, schools can lead the way to teach other social institutions how to arrest and reverse the injustices made worse by current events. This is a time for an urgent response. We intend for this book to be a call to action for educational, religious, civic, and private advocates at the local and national levels to engage in, commit to, and address the urgent challenges ahead of us.

A book can be seen as simply one's point of view . . . as ideas on a page. We intend for this book to be a clarion call to move beyond words and bold conversations to action, and we invite our readers to join us on the journey. In addition to presenting a call to action, another important purpose of this book is to provide educational leaders with a lens, a framework, and a set of tools to assess and address educational inequities in communities today. We acknowledge the many leaders who already are on board and skilled for this work, but we also recognize that the work is hard and that even the loudest, most capable advocates need new conversations, fresh ideas and approaches, and renewed motivation to bolster their work. The final purpose of this book is to create an ongoing community of bold thinkers and activists to share and support each other in this work. We do not know all there is to know; however, we have learned many things on our journeys. We know things now that we did not know ten years ago, and we look forward to sharing those lessons with you. We will enhance the tools we share with our readers with lived lessons and perspectives from our work in the field and personal case stories. We invite you to apply your own knowledge and analyses to further inform and contribute to the collective knowledge we all need to sustain this work. This is work that calls for all of us to come together to share ideas and best practices to support each other through difficult times. We welcome you on board!

We introduced readers to the Culturally Proficient Framework and tools in our first book. The framework is an organizer for understanding how to use four specific tools of Cultural Proficiency to begin and guide your work for creating and sustaining equity-based practices in your organizations. Chapter 2 will review the framework and tools in an updated context.

Furthermore, readers may recall that this work begins and is sustained with a mind shift that reflects how people think, talk, and act in an emerging equity culture. One of the guiding principles of Cultural Proficiency states, "People are served in varying degrees by the dominant culture." This principle is important for us to understand as educators because it explains the beginnings of the access, achievement, and opportunity gaps that plague underserved communities across this nation. Narrowing and closing these gaps is the ultimate goal of Cultural Proficiency.

- The above guiding principle of Cultural Proficiency provides the moral imperative for conducting this work at both the personal and organizational levels.

- The Cultural Proficiency Continuum and, specifically in this book, the Cultural Proficiency Leadership Rubric that we present and discuss in Chapters 3 and 4 give us a common language to discuss difficult, often controversial, topics in a non-contentious manner and provide examples of ineffective and effective practices to guide our transformation for inclusion and equity. This in turn stimulates conversation and provides a place for individuals of all backgrounds, racial groups, ethnicities, and identities to examine their personal and organizational positions on the continuum, assess the current status quo, and identify next steps to make progress toward Cultural Proficiency and closing educational gaps.

- Another tool, the five essential elements of Cultural Proficiency, provides behavioral standards to guide culturally competent leaders as they address current societal and organizational challenges. The five essential elements of Cultural Proficiency are as follows:
  - Assessing culture (one's own and others)
  - Valuing diversity
  - Managing the dynamics of difference
  - Adapting to diversity
  - Institutionalizing cultural knowledge

All the tools within the Culturally Proficient Framework, which we will discuss in more detail in Chapter 2, provide leaders with a toolkit for examining, discussing, and making changes to policies and practices to better meet the needs of communities during this historic time when there is a national effort to focus on issues of equity and inclusion. In addition, our lived experiences, as expressed in this book, can be used in training and staff development sessions to engage in constructive conversations about difficult and sensitive topics and to examine the particular applications of Cultural Proficiency as revealed in our case stories and the Cultural Proficiency Leadership Rubric in Chapter 4.

We begin by reintroducing ourselves and updating what has transpired in our professional lives in the past decade.

Carmella S. Franco completed her tenure as a state trustee of a takeover school district in Monterey County. Franco's work with governance has included districts with a majority of lower-socioeconomic, underserved students. She is recognized for assisting districts that are experiencing difficult situations. Professional presentations with co-authors Ott and Robles and others have centered on advancing the numbers of women of color in leadership positions throughout the country. She serves as a superintendents' coach and adviser and a mentor to aspiring superintendents of color for a number of organizations, including the AASA-USC Rossier Urban Superintendents Academy.

Maria G. Ott joined the University of Southern California Rossier School of Education as a faculty member upon retirement from the superintendency and currently holds the Irving R. and Virginia A. Melbo Chair in Education Administration. Her transition to higher education was an opportunity to prepare leaders for school systems, higher education, and organizations serving society in the nonprofit and for-profit environments. Ott designed and launched the AASA-USC Rossier Urban Superintendents Academy in 2015 to prepare diverse and equity-minded leaders for K–12 system leadership. She is recognized for her leadership and advocacy for bilingual education, leadership development for women, and public-private partnerships in education, and serves as a board member for the Association of Latino Administrators and Superintendents (ALAS).

Darline P. Robles was a superintendent for twenty years. With her last appointment, she served as superintendent of the Los Angeles County Office of Education, the largest educational service region in the country. She left the superintendency to join the faculty at the Rossier School of Education, University of Southern California, to create a new master's in education focused on K–12 leadership and preparation for the administrator's credential. She also serves as the associate dean for Equity and Community Engagement, where she provides support and training to faculty and staff on issues of access, diversity, equity, and inclusion. Additionally, she is the diversity liaison to the university and is a member of the university's Cultural Journey Network. She continues to teach in the K–12 and higher education doctoral program focused on preparing school leaders to become strategic leaders with an equity mindset.

We are not the same leaders/authors of our first book. As you will read, what we know now that we didn't know then has fortified our approach and emboldened our message. We hope that our experiences and lessons will unfold in such a way to not only guide your progress but accelerate it as we share with you things we wish we knew when we began this journey ten years ago. The rest of this book provides further insight into the following ten lessons that we share with our readers.

1. The status quo and the false belief in a meritocracy work against inclusivity in all sectors of society, not just education.

2. Equity issues are civil rights issues; it is your duty as a public servant to confront them and help make lasting change.

3. Develop an anti-racist stance. Anti-racism is not the same thing as not being racist. Confront all forms of oppression, not just those that you know or care about the most. Create understanding about the generational trauma, bigotry, and oppression of all oppressed groups, including LGBTQ and gender-fluid populations.

4. Step out of your comfort zone. Confront racism and oppression and other brutal facts directly. Do not obfuscate issues with rhetoric or politically correct language. Support claims with data, not predominance of opinion. Advocacy is required of all equity leaders. Often activism is needed. Expect pushback and criticism. Do not try to avoid it; manage it. Accept the consequences of bold action, but seek support from key constituents ahead of time and during your equity campaign.

5. Assume everyone's best intentions, but make sure committees and decision-making groups share appropriate representation from the communities you serve to ensure that groups' issues are not misrepresented, silenced, or ignored.

(Continued)

(Continued)

6. Examine your own cultural identity(s), i.e., cultural membership and status, as an ongoing process. Who are your allies, and whom do you unintentionally oppress with your ignorance, words, thoughts, or actions? Take responsibility for challenging your own shortcomings and biases. Consider the extent to which you, yourself, are an obstacle to change.

7. Expect fatigue and battle scars. Address your emotional needs and the emotional needs of friends and colleagues who help you do this work. Have mentors and allies to guide and support you. Take informed risks. Do not be afraid to make and admit mistakes.

8. Develop the next generation of leaders. By developing leadership in others, you demonstrate effective executive leadership yourself, and you establish the groundwork for institutionalizing change across the organization.

9. Understand that becoming culturally proficient is not just something you do at work. It is a lifelong personal experience for evolving your humanity on this planet. Embrace the process. Just because you will never finish the work does not mean you are excused from starting it.

10. Becoming culturally proficient is an inside-out approach. It is not something the leader does *to* others, nor is it something they delegate. The executive leader holds and communicates the vision for the work, directs the work, understands the work, participates in the work, and is ultimately responsible for the outcomes.

CHAPTER 2

....

CULTURAL PROFICIENCY

The Conceptual Framework and Tools

"If you want to teach people a new way of thinking, don't bother trying to teach them. Instead, give them a tool, the use of which will lead to new ways of thinking."

R. Buckminster Fuller

We have written this book to provide you with a way to apply some of the learning from *A Culturally Proficient Society Begins in School: Leadership for Equity* (Franco et al., 2011). In that book, we used our personal stories and experiences to chronicle our journeys to becoming among the very first female Latina urban superintendents of our generation. Our stories, replete with trials and tribulations, opportunities and setbacks, resources and lack of them, mentors and detractors, best-laid plans, and detours, were also suffused with many barriers and incidents of discrimination that might have derailed our trajectories but did not. We survived. We overcame! We celebrate every painful and joyful experience that contributed to our success. Hemingway (1929) wrote in *A Farewell to Arms* that "the world breaks everyone and afterward many are strong in the broken places." Although we are now stronger in our broken places, the discrimination we encountered on our paths echoes palpably every time we encounter similar situations in classrooms and schools, where it is obvious that some students and parents are valued less than others, and in the disparity of educational outcomes that separate poor children and children of color from their white and middle-class peers. Getting strong in our broken places had a lot to do with who we were at the core. Our cultural identities as Latinas and women taught us to survive with grace. One of the lessons we shared in our first book was how important our cultures were in shaping how we see others and ourselves—how we think, learn, communicate, teach, and lead. Our cultural identities define how we celebrate, love, and grieve. The intersection of who we are as women and who we are as Latinas has always been a pillar of strength to support us along the way and the main influence on our classroom and leadership pedagogies. The formidable role that culture plays for us is often absent for members of the dominant culture, who may not understand why we must define ourselves as Latina superintendents and not just superintendents. We cannot separate who we are from our struggles and our many first-generation accomplishments. We cannot see ourselves as just successful educational leaders without first considering who and what and how we are in this world. In sharing our stories about the formative role culture plays in our lives, we found kindred spirits with similar stories, challenges, and questions about the correlation between culture and educational success. While much research has been published about the culture and learning connection, none of it suggests causality. Yet many cannot help believing that poor children, children of color, and non-English-speaking children are simply fated to fail and that pouring resources into some demographic groups is an investment with little or no return. Still, while there is no causation, there is a disturbing correlation between who kids are and how they perform in school. Year after year, studies reveal that some students who start school with less of everything are given even less in school, as if they do not deserve it or we cannot justify offering the best resources to help them succeed.

One of the requirements of using Cultural Proficiency (Cross et al., 1989; Lindsey et al., 2009, 2013; Nuri-Robins, 2011) as a lens to examine and address inequity in schools is that we not see community members as underperforming but rather as underserved by a system that does not have the will or the skill to meet their learning needs. This lens forces us to examine what *we*, not *they*, can do differently to close gaps. Cultural Proficiency does not blame others for their lack of progress. Instead, it points the finger back at those in the system who must take responsibility for the many intentional and unintentional policies, decisions, and actions that impede educational progress for some students. We are adding to the conversation the perspective that when we focus on our practice as educational leaders, we can make a difference for all our students and their communities *if* we pay attention to who our students are and what their particular needs are, rather than our needs or the needs of the school system.

THE CONCEPTUAL FRAMEWORK AS A GUIDE: THE FOUR TOOLS OF CULTURAL PROFICIENCY

The purpose of this chapter is to explore Cultural Proficiency as a lens, a framework, and a set of tools to begin the work of both examining our current practices and planning for system-wide changes to create and sustain equity-driven systems that better meet the needs of *all* students, not just those whose backgrounds, experiences, opportunities, and resources better prepare them for school.

Cultural Proficiency helps us examine where we are, where we are not, and where we would like to be to better meet community members' needs. Cultural Proficiency is a mindset, a worldview. Those who commit to culturally proficient practices experience a paradigmatic shift from viewing others as problematic to viewing how one works with people different from oneself in a manner that ensures effective practices and outcomes. Cultural Proficiency is composed of an interrelated set of four tools, which, when used authentically, provide the opportunity to improve one's own practice in service of others. The tools of Cultural Proficiency are *not* strategies or techniques. They are guides to provide you with the means to examine and perform your professional responsibilities in a culturally proficient manner. Yet you can perform tasks related to educator functions and never utter the words *Cultural Proficiency*. Cultural Proficiency is about being effective in cross-cultural situations. In the context of schools, Cultural Proficiency is foremost about being effective in educating *all* students. It is also about respect for diversity, inclusion, successful cross-cultural communication, and relationships. But if disparate results exist between some demographic groups, then it is obvious that we are ineffective in handling diversity, inclusion, and cross-cultural communication. Therefore, while the optics of having vision statements and goals about "diversity" or "inclusion" are politically helpful, such goals do not mean a thing if we are not narrowing and closing the chronic, pernicious educational gaps (access, opportunity, and achievement gaps) that exist disproportionately for some student groups (students of color, students impacted by poverty, English-language learners, and special-needs students). These gaps are what racism and oppression look like in schools. The gaps are fueled by the policies and practices, values, and beliefs that well-meaning individuals like you and us mete out daily. Cultural Proficiency forces us to start our work by examining the self and our own organizational practice. What do our data say? What are our gaps? Between and among what groups? Let us be clear: Cultural Proficiency is not about improvement or getting better; better than what? The only thing that moves us further toward

Cultural Proficiency is narrowing and closing the gaps. From an equity standpoint, improvement does not matter if gaps are not closing.

Because we must start this work by examining our own values, beliefs, and practices, Cultural Proficiency also is not something we immediately unload onto others. It starts with the leaders, not the people they hire and supervise. Therefore, another requirement of Cultural Proficiency work is that we understand it is an *inside-out* process in which a person is, first and foremost, a student of their own assumptions, beliefs, and actions. We apply this inside-out process to examine school policies and practices that either impede or facilitate equity. And we need not be defensive when we discover that we, with all our best intentions, might actually be in the way of progress. Cultural Proficiency provides a comprehensive, systemic structure for school leaders to discuss difficult, often controversial issues facing schools today. The four tools of Cultural Proficiency provide educators with the means to assess and change their own values and behaviors and school policies and practices in ways that serve all students and, therefore, eventually our society. Cultural Proficiency has little to do with the outcomes we *intend* and everything to do with the outcomes we *actually get*.

Cultural Proficiency also is not necessarily something new to put on our already overflowing plates. It is a lens through which we see all the work we currently do and must do. It is possible to take the journey to Cultural Proficiency without a formal plan because we already have numerous plans that guide our work, and it is easy enough to simply shift our focus and our mindset and envision different outcomes, *outcomes for equity*, for the plans we already have in place.

In this section, we summarize the salient feature of each of the four tools of Cultural Proficiency. The tools, organized into a framework, will guide your thinking and provide common language and concepts to make difficult conversations less contentious and help you move forward with intentionality for equity.

Figure 2.1 references the table in our book *A Culturally Proficient Society Begins in School: Leadership for Equity* (Franco et al., 2011, p. 61) and shows the four tools of Cultural Proficiency and their relationships to one another.

Begin by reading Figure 2.1 from the bottom up. The framework is built on understanding why you need to change and where and how you might encounter resistance for the work to begin. We often refer to the baseline organizational change that needs to take place as changing the mindset.

FIGURE 2.1 THE CULTURALLY PROFICIENT FRAMEWORK

The Five Essential Elements of Cultural Competence

Serve as standards for personal, professional values and behavior, as well as organizational policies and practices

- **Assessing cultural knowledge**
- **Valuing diversity**
- **Managing the dynamics of difference**
- **Adapting to diversity**
- **Institutionalizing cultural knowledge**

The Cultural Proficiency Continuum portrays people and organizations who possess the knowledge, skills, and moral bearing to distinguish among equitable and inequitable practices as represented by different worldviews:

Informs

Unhealthy, unproductive, and inequitable policies, practices, and behaviors	Differing Worldviews	**Healthy, productive, and equitable policies, practices, and behaviors**
• Cultural destructiveness • Cultural incapacity • Cultural blindness		• Cultural precompetence • Cultural competence • Cultural Proficiency

Informs

Resolving the tension to do what is socially just within our diverse society leads people and organizations to view selves in terms productive and equitable.

Informs

Overcoming Barriers to Cultural Proficiency

Serve as personal, professional, and institutional impediments to moral and just service to a diverse society by:

- being resistant to change,
- being unaware of the need to adapt,
- not acknowledging systemic oppression, and
- benefiting from a sense of privilege and entitlement.

Ethical Tension

Guiding Principles of Cultural Proficiency

Provide a moral framework for conducting one's self and organization in an ethical fashion by believing the following:

- Culture is a predominant force in society.
- People are served in varying degrees by the dominant culture.
- People have individual and group identities.
- Diversity within cultures is vast and significant.
- Each cultural group has unique cultural needs.
- The best of both worlds enhances the capacity of all.
- The family, as defined by each culture, is the primary system of support in the education of children.
- School systems must recognize that marginalized populations have to be at least bicultural and that this status creates a distinct set of issues to which the system must be equipped to respond.
- Inherent in cross-cultural interactions are dynamics that must be acknowledged, adjusted to, and accepted.

SOURCE: Adapted from R. B. Lindsey, Nuri-Robins, and Terrell (2009, p. 60).

The Barriers to Cultural Proficiency

Our careers have been marked by both challenging and positive experiences. Some of the challenges have to do with the resistance we met along the way. As you read our case stories in Chapter 4, be mindful of the barriers we encountered and that you may also have experienced or are experiencing, as well as barriers that exist for students in your schools and districts. Recognizing why some stakeholders resist change helps the leader know how to challenge assumptions behind the resistance and inertia. These barriers manifest in the following stakeholder beliefs and actions.

Being resistant to change: We all have examples of this barrier. It manifests in organizations that have a culture of just doing the same thing, in the same way, year after year, despite changing demographics, changing societal events, or major educational reforms. Organizations tend to remain committed to the status quo unless forced to change. This barrier is often accompanied by an inherent mistrust in decisions made by top-level managers and governing agencies. Building trust and open communication are essential to counter this barrier.

Being unaware of the need to adapt: Constituents who are relatively satisfied with services from the schools tend to be those parents who feel that their children's needs are being met because they have access to additional resources and opportunities to augment what is offered. They may be unaware of changing demographics or performance data that correlate with demographic shifts, so they see no need to change. Sharing data and discussing their implications help alter this faulty perception.

Not acknowledging systemic oppression: This barrier often manifests in statements such as, "It is not I who needs to change," "I have been a successful educator for years," and "These kids/parents just need to get a clue!" This barrier arises when stakeholders believe in a meritocracy where everybody receives their just rewards according to what they "deserve." This belief comes from the notion that the world is fair and everybody has the same chance to succeed. Those who do not or cannot succeed are seen as not having worked hard enough or not being worthy or deserving of success through some fault of their own. Even if barriers for some students are perceived, allowing accommodations for them to be successful is resisted because doing so is seen as watering down standards and giving some people an unfair advantage.

Benefiting from a sense of privilege and entitlement: When some community members have cultural traits that align with the cultural traits of the school (for example, white, middle-class, English-language dominant, competitive, self-determined, and individualistic), they see no reason for schools to change. Classrooms taught in English with a pedagogy of individualism, competition, and survival of the fittest work quite well for some students. Some students and parents feel that structures such as cooperative learning and student-team-centered projects limit opportunities for students with dominant cultural traits to excel above the others. These students and parents resist practices to democratize the classroom because if they cannot compete or excel, they feel they have lost the leading edge they think they need to be successful in school and society. These ideas are often expressed by the loudest or most influential stakeholders, who can and do block changes that do not benefit people like them.

Regardless of which kinds of barriers leaders encounter, they must assess the extent to which the barrier is espoused by a few stakeholders or enough stakeholders to derail progress altogether. Educators must engage in intentional conversations about how parents and students who are different from them interact and learn. Educators must also use data to *tell the truth* about the extent to which public schools are educating all children to high standards. Cultural Proficiency is an approach for public entities to examine their effectiveness in advancing the public good. Sharing data with the educational community about schools' effectiveness in educating all students surfaces assumptions and values about which students succeed and which do not. This awareness can unblock resistance as people gain more understanding and some degree of compassion for community members who have unique and valuable differences compared with dominant groups.

The Guiding Principles of Cultural Proficiency

The guiding principles of Cultural Proficiency help you know and understand how people think, talk, and act when a culturally proficient mindset is emerging within yourself and your organization. They provide a framework for examining and understanding the core values of individuals and schools making a mind shift for equity. The guiding principles and school-based examples of each one are as follows:

- *Culture is a predominant force in society.*

  <u>Illustrations</u>: Holidays, religious observances, heroes, and sports interests are examples of culture that affect educators, students, and parents. For

some, often members of disenfranchised groups, culture is a defining aspect of their identity. Those who do not define themselves by their racial/ethnic identity may still ascribe to some group that defines them, such as retired, vegan, baby boomers, Gen Xers, athletes, musicians, and so forth. In other words, it is human nature to look for and identify with groups that we feel help define who we are.

- *People are served in varying degrees by the dominant culture.*

  <u>Illustrations</u>: Those represented in the curriculum, achievement gains, and college and university enrollment are examples of those best served by the dominant culture, and those same individuals continue to prevail in establishing the purpose of school, writing curricula and textbooks, defining proficiency levels, and continuing to represent the predominant culture(s) working in schools. Furthermore, the school calendar, instructional materials and methodologies, the language of instruction, assessment options, the way we reach out to parents, the faces and stories in textbooks, and even the food in the cafeteria are all examples of how schools serve some cultural groups better than others.

- *People have individual and group identities.*

  <u>Illustrations</u>: Each educator, parent, guardian, student, and community member is an individual person with an identity that makes them unique. At the same time, they have gender identity, have sexual orientation, may be a member of a religious group, know their racial/ethnic background, and most likely are a member of other formal and informal groups. In our elementary schools, we know that elementary students have different needs from high school students, but within those large groups, we can further identify the needs of second graders as different from those of fifth graders. And even among all second graders, there are myriad individual needs.

- *Diversity within cultures is vast and significant.*

  <u>Illustrations</u>: Latinx, African American, European American, Asian Pacific Islander, and other racial/ethnic groups are not monolithic. Within each larger group, there are numerous sub-ethnic, dialectical, religious, gender, social class, economic, sexual orientation, and generational classifications with which people can and do identify. Within school districts, we often speak of the organizational cultural differences among schools or among the grade levels or departments within the same school.

- *Each cultural group has unique cultural needs.*

  <u>Illustrations</u>: The varied and intersectional cultures that schools serve have varied learning needs. Home experiences, traditions, rituals,

holidays, and generational and gender roles differ from culture to culture and within the same culture. These must be acknowledged and understood by staff who want to better understand and meet families' needs.

- *The best of both worlds enhances the capacity of all.*

  Illustrations: Being bicultural is an asset. It develops abilities and capacities in the student that can enhance learning. Students need to feel like they belong in both cultures, and they and their parents need to be acknowledged and valued for what they *do* know and *can* do and how such knowledge and ability can enhance student success in school.

- *The family, as defined by each culture, is the primary system of support in the education of children.*

  Illustrations: Often grandparents, aunts, or older siblings of children with working or absent parents attend school meetings and take part in follow-up. Same-sex parents, foster parents, co-custodians, and parents who are temporarily incarcerated, in rehabilitation, or absent are still parents and should be acknowledged as such and deserve to be involved in the education of their children.

- *School systems must recognize that marginalized populations have to be at least bicultural and that this status creates a distinct set of issues to which the system must be equipped to respond.*

  Illustrations: Often students must attend school and other meetings with parents to translate for them. Schools must realize that children may play the role of adult or caretaker to parents who do not speak English or know how to navigate complicated systems like health care, the motor vehicle department, and/or insurance requirements. These roles compete with students' study and homework time. To feel empowered and see themselves in both cultures, children must retain ties to the home culture, values, beliefs, and language(s) while learning to become competent in the culture and language of schools. These children are multitasking, and schools need to understand the stress and complexity of some students' lives and that the cultural knowledge children have and their ability to multitask are assets for learning.

- *Inherent in cross-cultural interactions are dynamics that must be acknowledged, adjusted to, and accepted.*

  Illustrations: Dimensions of culture vary from group to group. Some cultures desire children to be compliant at school, while teachers may expect active involvement, initiative, and competition. Hierarchical structures at home may conflict with blurred expectations for gender roles and authority figures at school. Parents may prefer their children to follow the rules, be good, be helpful, and be courteous, as opposed to teachers who expect students to be inquisitive, competitive, and self-reliant. Neither is more correct than the other. Schools need to honor all styles and use them as assets in the learning process.

Read the guiding principles. To what extent do you and your colleagues believe these principles? They are the foundation for your work. If you cannot believe them or cannot get buy-in from a critical mass of stakeholders in your organization, your progress may be delayed. Notice the principle that states, "People are served in varying degrees by the dominant culture." Some may balk at the term *dominant culture,* but when you think about it, there are many vestiges and manifestations of the dominant culture in schools today that we take for granted, such as the language of instruction; the stories, people, and events in our textbooks; the food in the cafeteria; the school calendar; our system of teaching and grading; and the diversity of the staff, just to name a few. No one wants to assume that these structures were invented to dominate or harm some students, but no one can deny that many of these structures do, in fact, benefit some students and parents more than others. Hence, *people are served to varying degrees by the dominant culture.* Here is where educational gaps begin: where some students benefit more than others from the school experience. While you cannot require people to believe in these principles, you can facilitate a greater understanding of them over time. Do not underestimate the importance of having those with whom you work understand and buy in to these principles. Before the planning stage, before making programmatic changes, it is important to share data, have cross-group conversations, and offer various equity-based training opportunities to create an understanding of these principles, which creates the readiness for Cultural Proficiency work. Please note the zone of *ethical tension* between the barriers and the guiding principles in Figure 2.1. Being able to accept the beliefs exemplified by the guiding principles enables leaders to want and begin to transform systems for equity. Not being able to accept the beliefs exemplified by the guiding principles forces leaders into a situation of believing that those who are underperforming are to blame for their lack of progress and must either make changes themselves to better access the resources and opportunities schools offer or forever have limited access to success. The tension is extant in those who are eager to transform for equity versus those who can barely tolerate diversity. This is the pivot point where leaders have two stark choices:

- We choose to stay stuck in the inertia of believing either in cultural deficit theory or, every bit as damaging, the intractability of systemic oppression.

- We choose to believe in the guiding principles and in *our capacity to do whatever it takes* to make changes that benefit historically underserved students and their parents.

The Cultural Proficiency Continuum

The Cultural Proficiency Continuum provides specific descriptions of both unhealthy, unproductive, and inequitable as compared with healthy, productive, and equitable *policies, practices, and behaviors* of individuals and organizations. In addition, the continuum can help you assess your current state and project your desired state. In this manner, it is a model for change. Movement along the continuum is the goal and represents paradigmatic shifts in thinking. The illustrations are not unique; they are samples, and any other examples could substitute as long as they portray the general worldview of that point along the continuum (from *cultural destructiveness* to *Cultural Proficiency*). Often the continuum becomes the tool that practitioners find most practical in guiding their work, as it can be valuable in showing forward progress. However, the continuum is not all there is to the work. Neither can the continuum be useful unless users understand the pillars on which it is based and how the other tools inform it. Note that the three points on the left side of the continuum (i.e., *cultural destructiveness, cultural incapacity, cultural blindness*) focus on *the others* as being problematic, and the three points on the right of the continuum (i.e., *cultural precompetence, cultural competence, Cultural Proficiency*) focus on *us* or our *practices*. Culturally destructive, incapable, and blind behaviors demonstrate attitudes about how students (or other groups) are blamed for their lack of progress or success and referred to as *underperforming*, while the next three points—culturally precompetent, competent, and proficient behaviors—demonstrate how educators and leaders refer to the ways people and practices *underserve* our students and their communities. The six points on the continuum are these:

- *Cultural destructiveness—see the difference; stomp it out.* Seeking to eliminate vestiges of the others' cultures. Often these attitudes and behaviors are intentional.

  Illustrations: Historical examples include the system of slavery, the westward expansion of the United States that resulted in the near extinction of First Nations, and the presence of school curricula that seek to ignore these and other egregious acts in our history. Modern examples range from physical acts such as gay bashing to educational practices that perpetuate generational underachievement of demographic groups. Other examples include missing or distorted histories of some groups in the curricula and textbooks, the chronic under-education and miseducation of children of color, and the limited life-affirming options for such children beyond school.

- *Cultural incapacity—see the difference; make it wrong.* Intentional or non-intentional practices that exclude, disrespect, disempower, or limit access for some cultural groups.

  Illustrations: Historical examples include legislation such as immigrant exclusion laws that severely curtailed Asian immigration, the executive order that remanded U.S. citizens of Japanese ancestry into "relocation camps" during World War II, and law-based discriminatory hiring practices used throughout our country until the late half of the twentieth century. Current school-oriented examples include the expressed assumption that parents from some cultural groups do not care about their children's education if they do not come to school events, or the belief that students who are not fluent in English cannot learn or require low-level materials. Most recently, during the closure of schools due to the COVID-19 pandemic, many students in need lost access to resources and services they depended on for online learning, nutritional well-being, and mental health. Even providing computers for online learning was not nearly enough for some students and parents who needed the other support services that kept students safe and healthy. These good intentions based on a recognition of what was needed by most students just did not go far enough for some students, and the result was that too many students were, in fact, punished during the pandemic by losing access to school support services. Therefore, too many students who were already struggling in school fell far behind their peers and are unable to catch up to this day.

- *Cultural blindness—see the difference; act like you don't.* Refusing to acknowledge the cultures of others, and promoting the belief that everyone is served equally by the same policies and practices.

  Illustrations: Historical examples include the failure to recognize or even see the artistic, athletic, economic, and political accomplishments of women, nondominant ethnic groups, and LGBTQ individuals. Cultural blindness is represented by colleagues who profess to be color-blind and are, therefore, unaware of learning barriers and achievement gaps that exist for some groups, or see the learning barriers but are not willing to make accommodations for some students, thinking it provides an unfair advantage to them.

- *Cultural precompetence—see the difference; maybe or maybe not respond appropriately.* This level of behavior on the continuum acknowledges that people recognize that they do not know everything there is to know about working in diverse settings. At this level, we see initial levels of "recognition" about gaps, after which an individual/organization can move in a positive, constructive direction, or they can falter, stop, and possibly regress. Often at this level, leaders who are anxious to know what they do not know seek one-shot, short-lived, quick-fix programs or opportunities with promising outcomes but limited results for closing gaps. Or they may order such professional development for staff but not attend themselves. Disillusioned by hard work or stalled efforts, leaders may regress to old ways or look outside of themselves for other "silver bullet" solutions, which never materialize. The work is *inside-out*, meaning it starts on the inside, by examining the self, one's own professional practices, and one's own organizational data, not by first reaching out to outside experts or programs. External supports will eventually enhance your work, but the first steps start with examining the self and one's readiness and capacity for knowing and serving others better.

Illustrations: In our recent past, there have been numerous attempts to address the needs of underachieving students that included "pullout programs," gender- or race-based academies, and other ability grouping that has led to tracking. The distinguishing characteristic of culturally precompetent educators who seek to learn how to best serve the needs of all students is that while they may implement programs that seem promising, they track progress and do not perpetuate approaches that fail to result in equitable outcomes. These leaders continue to research, learn, and implement practices to serve all students well and then share best practices with networks of like-minded colleagues also wanting to change the mindset for equity.

- *Cultural competence—see the difference; redress bias and inequity.* Behaviors at this level of the continuum intend to redress wrongs, reallocate resources, rebalance services offered, and accelerate progress for underserved students. The leader enters diverse settings in a manner that is additive to cultures that are different from their own while learning about and evolving their understanding about their own cultural identity and status to adapt to meet the needs of others.

Illustrations: Examples include educators who acknowledge changing demographics in their schools and adapt the curriculum and instructional practices to "recognize and respond" to students in classrooms today, not the ones who used to attend our schools. In these classrooms and schools, culture is a normal part of educator conversations. Educators make cultural and linguistic adaptations to curriculum, instruction, and assessment. Textbooks, materials, and public resources will abound with diverse images, including those of groups who are not members of the current student population.

- *Cultural Proficiency—see the difference, esteem the difference, and advocate for equity.* Behaviors at this level of the continuum intend to and do rebalance or re-level power dynamics and relationships in schools and in other institutions in society. Educators and leaders make the commitment to lifelong learning for the purpose of being increasingly effective in serving the educational needs of current cultural groups while keeping an eye on making adaptations needed to meet the needs of future students.

  Illustrations: Educators who strive to achieve Cultural Proficiency recognize and value professional development for themselves and their colleagues, are activistic in their advocacy, and have the will "to do whatever it takes" to close gaps and make education a truly inclusive and democratic enterprise where no one is left on the margins and everyone has the optimal opportunity to participate in meaningful ways in a just society.

Cultural Proficiency continua or rubrics have been developed to examine equitable practices in specific areas of education, such as curriculum and instruction, assessment and accountability, parent and community engagement, professional development, and educational social justice, to name a few.

The Five Essential Elements of Cultural Competence

The *five essential elements of cultural competence* represent five distinct areas of practice to help us further organize, understand, and navigate the continuum. The five essential elements are behavioral standards or skill sets that can be observed in individuals or organizations that begin to develop the changing mindset for cultural competence. They represent values, behaviors, policies, and practices that hold us accountable for doing deep transformation work that changes outcomes for underserved clients. Typically, these standards or skills are most observable at the fifth level of the continuum, or *cultural competence*. The five essential elements are as follows:

- *Assessing cultural knowledge*—Being aware of what you know about others' cultures and your own, how you react to differences in others' cultures, and what you do to be effective in cross-cultural situations.

- *Valuing diversity*—Making the effort to be inclusive of people whose viewpoints and experiences are different from yours and that will enrich conversations, decision-making, and problem-solving.

- *Managing the dynamics of difference*—Viewing conflict as a natural and normal process that often has cultural contexts that can be understood to enhance cross-group communication and trust-building. Managing the dynamics of difference helps leaders use conflict for constructive and supportive problem-solving rather than being intimidated by it.

- *Adapting to diversity*—Having the will to learn about others and the ability to use others' cultural experiences and backgrounds in educational settings. This essential element means being able to adapt to the cultural needs of others instead of expecting others to adapt to your needs.

- *Institutionalizing cultural knowledge*—Learning about one's own culture(s) and the culture(s) of others and their experiences, perspectives, and needs is an integral part of individual and organizational lifelong learning to hold individuals and organizations accountable to effectively meet the needs of the current public with an eye toward the future and changing demographics and needs.

In the next chapter, we will introduce a continuum and five essential elements tailored specifically to guide leaders in their practice. The Cultural Proficiency Leadership Rubric integrates the six levels of Cultural Proficiency discussed above with the five essential elements or standards of Cultural Proficiency. In addition to sharing the specific Cultural Proficiency Leadership Rubric with our readers in Chapter 3, we will use it to analyze four authentic case stories in Chapter 4 to contextualize the theoretical nature of this tool in real-life professional settings.

REFLECTION: OVERALL

- How comfortable are you with your knowledge about Cultural Proficiency? What questions do you have? How do you see the tools helping you and members of your school community narrow and close educational gaps?

_____

_____

_____

_____

- What conversations do you need to start with your school community?

_____

_____

_____

_____

- What partners or support networks will you seek to begin this work?

_____

_____

_____

_____

REFLECTIONS: BARRIERS
....

- What barriers are preventing you from starting your Cultural Proficiency work? How will you begin to eliminate those barriers?

_____

_____

_____

_____

REFLECTIONS: GUIDING PRINCIPLES
....

- To what extent do people on your staff believe or buy in to the guiding principles of Cultural Proficiency? Considering the principle *People are served to varying degrees by the dominant culture,* to what extent do people you work with know this? How can you increase their awareness of it? Given that they know it, to what extent do they care enough about this principle to do something about it? How can you demonstrate more concern and interest about this guiding principle?

_____

_____

_____

_____

REFLECTIONS: CULTURAL PROFICIENCY CONTINUUM

- Given that we can be at different levels on the Cultural Proficiency Continuum depending on various diversity issues, where on the continuum do you think you fall, overall? Where does your organization fall, overall? How might you use the continuum to build knowledge and capacity among stakeholders in your educational community?

_____

_____

_____

_____

REFLECTIONS: FIVE ESSENTIAL ELEMENTS OF CULTURAL COMPETENCE

- Which elements are most visible in your practice? In the practices of others? How can you build capacity for more people to embrace and use the essential elements?

_____

_____

_____

_____

CHAPTER 3

....

THE EXECUTIVE LEADERSHIP RUBRIC

Lessons From the Field

"A child in India grows up with the idea that you have to make choices that will create a better future. In fact, your whole life is a continuum of choices, so the more conscious you are, the greater your life will be."

Deepak Chopra

In the ten years since we wrote our first book, the world has changed in significant ways, and education has responded with its concomitant spate of legislation, reforms, resource allocation, and reallocation. A global pandemic challenged states and school districts to suspend or scrap policies and practices that had taken years to research and implement. Schooling, as we knew it, was turned upside down. Unfortunately, one thing did not change and may have gotten worse: disproportional educational gaps persist. During the pandemic, we let some students slip through the cracks even further. Many students who once benefited from being in the safe, stable, predictable environments of classrooms and schools—receiving two meals a day under the watchful eye of caring adults—were left to fend for themselves, often at home alone or watching siblings, with little if any access to nutritious meals. Staying on track with online learning was difficult, if not impossible. Unless we step forward to take radical steps to help these students catch up, educationally and socially, they will be permanently left behind.

In the context of historical, political, and cultural upheaval reflected in movements such as Black Lives Matter and #MeToo, many people have finally come to realize how inequity in society and its institutions affects some people more than others. Those people seem ready to engage in action for social justice. Yet others have come to define themselves by confronting any progress made for social justice and aiming to stop or reverse it. The safeguards of our Constitution are at risk. There can be no liberty in the absence of justice, and since social injustice begins with educational inequity, this is the time for educational leaders to take concerted action to expose and identify the root causes of inequity in schools, to narrow and close educational gaps, or in time to provide the leadership to confront the power structures that stem from them.

To delve deeper into the issues discussed above, this chapter is designed to connect our professional experiences with two of the tools of Cultural Proficiency, to demystify the tools and accelerate your use of them. One of the tools we introduced earlier was the Cultural Proficiency Continuum, which we defined as a model for change that provides specific descriptions of unhealthy and healthy values, behaviors, practices, and policies of individuals and organizations on the way to Cultural Proficiency. Table 3.1 presents a specific kind of Cultural Proficiency continuum: one that will help us examine beliefs, values, and actions of educational leaders. We call it the Cultural Proficiency Leadership Rubric. We also refer to this tool as just the Cultural Proficiency Rubric. A *continuum* helps us examine practice as a progression of values over time or from one state to another. A *rubric* helps us assess our performance or progress against some standard. In this regard, the rubric does two things: it helps us assess where we are and where we want to go on our Cultural Proficiency journey, and it helps us know how complex or difficult the work will be. This specific Cultural Proficiency Leadership Rubric uses two tools in an interrelated fashion to help you start your work. The two tools are the continuum itself, with six vertical columns or levels of culturally proficient behaviors, and the five essential elements, which you will recall as the five standards of practice that further help us and others understand how to think and act as we make progress along the continuum.

The examples offered in the cells are just that, and any number of other examples might be equally good to illuminate the continuum. In fact, we invite our readers to identify situations, policies, or behaviors that might fit into various cells of the Cultural Proficiency Leadership Rubric. This is work that can be started on your own or with a small group of committed colleagues with whom you feel comfortable sharing thoughts and observations about findings that might be troubling or controversial.

Let us take a look at the specific application of this tool. Please use this guide for reading and interpreting Table 3.1, the Cultural Proficiency Leadership Rubric:

- Note that the rubric is composed of rows and columns.

- There are seven columns. Columns two through seven are the levels or phases of the Cultural Proficiency Continuum (*destructiveness* through *proficiency*). The horizontal cells, or rows, help us locate personal or organizational behaviors, from destructive to proficient. The first vertical column sorts those behaviors into five essential elements, or the five standards of practice, which help you further identify how you should be thinking or acting as you move from the left side of the continuum or rubric to the right side. These five essential elements are further broken down in this continuum for a total of eleven possible sub-standards of behavior to analyze across the levels of the continuum. The essential element of "assessing cultural knowledge" has two sub-points, "valuing diversity" has two sub-points, "managing the dynamics of difference" has two sub-points, "adapting to difference" has three sub-points, and "institutionalizing cultural knowledge" has two sub-points. There are seventy-seven cells in this rubric. Remember, they are only samples, and we invite you to fill in other cells and/or add to the examples we provide. In Chapter 4, we will provide specific, real-world case stories to further illustrate how the continuum and the five essential elements can be used to analyze your progress and plan for actual transformation.

- Note that the sixth column is titled "Cultural Competence." The language in that column is in active voice and describes actions that can be taken today in schools. Cultural competence is most often our goal. We can assume that in most cases, the desired standard for Cultural Proficiency has been reached at the level of cultural competence.

- The seventh column is titled "Cultural Proficiency." The descriptions in this column are future-focused. We may catch glimpses of this level in discrete actions by individuals—or, at times, the entire organization— but these descriptions are most often ideals: highly evolved actions or future aspects of behavior. This last column or level reminds us not to get complacent even when we have made verifiable progress. We must keep our eye on the future. The last level of Cultural Proficiency pulls us beyond the plateau of current success to a horizon of what we need to anticipate, prepare for, and do to ensure that equity in schools and social justice in our communities can be sustained over time.

TABLE 3.1 THE CULTURAL PROFICIENCY LEADERSHIP RUBRIC

ASSESSING CULTURAL KNOWLEDGE	CULTURAL DESTRUCTIVENESS	CULTURAL INCAPACITY	CULTURAL BLINDNESS	CULTURAL PRECOMPETENCE	CULTURAL COMPETENCE	CULTURAL PROFICIENCY
The extent to which the leader uses personal experience to develop, maintain, and provoke a moral imperative (passion, knowledge, wisdom, diligence, and courage) for making positive changes that benefit underserved stakeholders in schools and in the community	Leaders rely on a narrow definition of "American culture" to develop and justify policies and procedures and resource allocation to those they believe are more entitled or capable than others to receive those resources, while denying or restricting resources to those deemed "unworthy" or incapable of achieving success in America.	Leaders tolerate diversity in schools but believe that the perspectives and attributes of the dominant culture are superior to those of other cultures. This belief justifies policies and practices that maintain the status quo and benefit those who reflect the attributes of the *dominant* culture, while limiting the leaders' motivation and resolve to make changes to benefit underserved stakeholders.	Leaders demonstrate managerial competence by supporting and being supported by agency policies and practices that promote a culture of continuous improvement for all students regardless of their cultural backgrounds and experiences. Evidence of effectiveness is limited to single measures such as agency-sanctioned standardized test scores, which reinforce the belief that "some students just do better than others."	Leaders are compassionate, caring, diligent professionals whose backgrounds compel a narrow focus on serving a particular cultural group, often the same culture as the leaders'. Such a focus may limit the leaders' cultural capacity to advocate for all underserved students and reinforces a belief that minority leaders are more capable of developing relationships with and addressing the needs of minority stakeholders.	Leaders are compassionate, diligent, and skilled professionals whose experiences have led to a profound understanding of long-term, systemic educational inequity. This understanding compels a relentless, fervent professional and personal commitment to challenge and break down barriers to educational access, opportunity, and success and close gaps for historically underserved stakeholders.	Leaders are compassionate, diligent, and transformational professionals who understand that inequities in school are a microcosm of inequities in society. Such understanding compels a relentless commitment to educating all stakeholders about educational and social injustice while also breaking down barriers to success for historically underserved stakeholders.

28

ASSESSING CULTURAL KNOWLEDGE	CULTURAL DESTRUCTIVENESS	CULTURAL INCAPACITY	CULTURAL BLINDNESS	CULTURAL PRECOMPETENCE	CULTURAL COMPETENCE	CULTURAL PROFICIENCY
The extent to which the leader perceives aspects of culture as assets and strengths (not deficits) to harness and optimize for effective teaching, learning, and leadership	Leaders believe that displays of culture are barriers to their own progress and the progress of others. Hence, such displays are repressed, discouraged, disparaged, or punished.	Leaders disavow the influence that culture has on learning and/ or their professional actions. They promote assimilation to the dominant culture of society, school, or the organization, often downplaying or hiding aspects of culture, believing them to reflect negatively on their leadership capacity and competence. Leaders promote programs that aim to remediate or assimilate underperforming students, limiting student access and progress and often exacerbating access and achievement gaps.	Leaders believe that culturally defined aspects such as motivation, talent, and diligence, not culture, influence learning, performance, and success. Focusing on aspects of culture is an unnecessary distraction or excuse for not learning or not being successful and may deter their advancement or promotion.	Leaders support programs, scholarships, networks, sponsorships, recruiting, hiring, promoting, and allocating resources for one or more cultural groups, but such resources may be single or short-term opportunities intended to ensure success for stakeholders who need ongoing support to navigate next steps toward success.	Leaders proudly assert their culture and culturally induced core values of courage, persistence, resiliency, risk-taking, and self-determination, while seeking and providing nurturing and supportive relationships, stewardship, and mentoring of other minority leaders and advocating for recruiting, hiring, and promoting of other minority leaders with the passion and capacity for closing equity gaps for underserved stakeholders.	Leaders from both minority and majority cultures understand how cultural identity (membership and status) can influence learning and success. Leaders embrace and leverage attributes of their own and others' cultures as assets to achieve organizational goals while accelerating progress and closing gaps for historically underserved groups in schools and in the community.

(Continued)

VALUING DIVERSITY	CULTURAL DESTRUCTIVENESS	CULTURAL INCAPACITY	CULTURAL BLINDNESS	CULTURAL PRECOMPETENCE	CULTURAL COMPETENCE	CULTURAL PROFICIENCY
The extent to which the leader is aware of, values, learns about, supports, and promotes their culture and the cultures of others	Leaders are fearful of or discouraged from promoting and demonstrating aspects of culture.	Leaders avoid referring to their own or other cultural perspectives and behaviors, and assimilate to the expected roles of the organization. Leaders expect others, including community members and students, to assimilate to be successful in school and in society.	Leaders do not believe there is any value in understanding culture to enhance or promote staff, leader, or student performance and success.	Leaders consider the cultural backgrounds of others when recruiting and hiring and may have been hired because of their cultural background, supporting a belief that minority-cultural-group staff and leaders are more capable of understanding and addressing cultural minority stakeholder needs and issues.	Leaders understand the influence of culture on learning, teaching, and leading, and promote culture as an asset to performance and success.	Leaders promote cultural pluralism as a way of meeting the needs of all stakeholders, not only those with the loudest voice, and to promote distribution of political, societal, and economic power among diverse groups, not just among an entitled electorate.
The extent to which the leader seeks, respects, and values multiple diverse ideas, opinions, cultural perspectives, experiences, and styles to inform decisions for the good of the organization and the community	Leaders promote/display dominant-group values and behaviors, ignoring or excluding diverse perspectives and often making decisions that benefit only stakeholders from the dominant culture.	Leaders solicit input and participation from diverse community members to comply with agency or funding source requirements for participation and representation of diverse groups.	Leaders believe their education and experience have adequately informed their decisions and actions. Soliciting community input is a polite political distraction but yields little toward attaining their leadership goals.	Leaders assign others or are assigned to work with stakeholders from their culture(s) because it is believed that being from a particular cultural group can better foster understanding, trust, and buy-in to the goals, policies, and decisions of the organization.	Leaders promote and model learning about the community in authentic ways for all stakeholders so the specific cultural perspectives, issues, and needs of all community groups can be better understood and addressed by all in the organization.	Leaders promote community building to exchange data and information to collaborate on common goals among disparate constituents and share resources for closing educational, societal, and economic gaps.

MANAGING THE DYNAMICS OF DIFFERENCE	CULTURAL DESTRUCTIVENESS	CULTURAL INCAPACITY	CULTURAL BLINDNESS	CULTURAL PRECOMPETENCE	CULTURAL COMPETENCE	CULTURAL PROFICIENCY
The extent to which the leader solicits diverse points of view, opinions, learning, communication, and leadership styles to promote flexibility in meeting organizational goals and to make decisions that reflect stakeholder issues.	Leaders make unilateral, authoritarian decisions with little or no input about stakeholder needs. Leaders may solicit particular perspectives to justify decisions or to withhold or deny programs, services, or resources to some stakeholders. Leaders' inflexibility and adherence to the structures and styles of the dominant organizational culture discourage participation of diverse stakeholders, leading to policies and practices that ignore or exclude their needs and issues.	Leaders may solicit input from diverse cultural groups, often only to comply with program regulations and not to incorporate diverse perspectives into decisions. Leaders attempting to manage the status quo and preserve tradition are not open to alternative ways to achieve goals and/or to meet the needs of diverse stakeholders. Hence, leaders make decisions or take action that misrepresents, disrespects, or trivializes the perspectives and issues of diverse stakeholders.	Leaders believe they are effective when they can prevent, mitigate, and avoid dissonance and conflict, especially conflict arising from diverse cultural perspectives. Few attempts are made to solicit diverse points of view, thereby reducing the opportunity for conflict and considerations of diverse perspectives. Leaders may facilitate consensus or bring multiple issues to a vote, often excluding diverse stakeholders' ideas and issues.	Leaders may consider input from majority stakeholder groups and/or one or few minority stakeholder groups, depending on which stakeholders proactively assert their ideas and opinions. Leaders may wrongly assume that stakeholders who do not come forward to make their needs known are satisfied with the status quo.	Leaders encourage diverse opinions and perspectives and facilitate conversations across cultures and viewpoints in productive, non-contentious, and non-polarizing ways. They engage in ongoing dialogue between and among groups to help the organization develop a customer-service orientation, and challenge the status quo by promoting organizational flexibility to meet diverse customer needs.	Leaders use conflict as a catalyst for dialogue to deepen personal, organizational, and community understanding about educational and societal injustice. Leaders use data to help stakeholders understand patterns of underperformance and underutilization of resources for some groups and to shift deficit thinking about diverse stakeholders to shared responsibility for better meeting their needs.

(Continued)

(Continued)

MANAGING THE DYNAMICS OF DIFFERENCE	CULTURAL DESTRUCTIVENESS	CULTURAL INCAPACITY	CULTURAL BLINDNESS	CULTURAL PRECOMPETENCE	CULTURAL COMPETENCE	CULTURAL PROFICIENCY
The extent to which the leader embraces risk to make decisions and take actions, which may not be popular with dominant cultures; anticipates criticism; persists in the face of criticism, inertia, barriers, or reversals; and accepts personal and professional consequences for advocating for underserved students and other stakeholders.	Leaders' ambiguity about who they are and why they are in the role results in passivity and conformity to low-level expectations and responsibility. Leaders lead without a moral purpose or imperative. In the face of conflict or criticism, leaders assert authority, withdraw from it, or totally ignore it.	Leaders from minority cultures are expected to maintain the status quo. Such leaders are professionally intimidated by taking risks or challenging the system. Innovation, creativity, and trailblazing are encouraged and rewarded for leaders from dominant groups to preserve a dominant cultural perspective in all leadership policies and practices.	Leaders believe it is organizationally expedient and encourage others to promote ideas and decisions that are popular and supported by the dominant or the majority groups, hence avoiding taking risks or being criticized for challenging the system.	Leaders take calculated risks, perhaps in favor of a particular issue or demographic group, but not consistently for all underserved stakeholders or for all issues that require advocacy from an organizational leader. Leaders avoid taking risks or being criticized if they perceive personal, professional, or political threats or negative consequences.	Leaders embrace risk and make decisions and take actions that may not be popular with dominant cultures. They anticipate criticism; persist in the face of criticism, inertia, barriers, or reversals; and accept personal and professional consequences for their advocacy for underserved students and other stakeholders.	Leaders embrace risk and criticism as necessary on their leadership journey and on their quest for what is right and just. Because failure is not an option and professional goals and personal goals are the same, persistence and progress—however challenged or challenging—empower leaders as lifetime agents for equity and social justice.

ADAPTING TO DIVERSITY	CULTURAL DESTRUCTIVENESS	CULTURAL INCAPACITY	CULTURAL BLINDNESS	CULTURAL PRECOMPETENCE	CULTURAL COMPETENCE	CULTURAL PROFICIENCY
The extent to which the leader facilitates an understanding about the truth of an organization's effectiveness in achieving equitable outcomes.	Leaders do not collect, share, or disaggregate data that show patterns of performance for underserved groups. Leaders may misuse disaggregated data to reinforce deficit perspectives about some students/parents to justify withholding resources for some groups. Data are used to conceal or manipulate the truth.	Leaders use data to develop programs and services that focus on interventions or remediation but limit student access to further learning opportunities needed for educational success or post-school options. Data are used to obscure the truth and serve the organization's needs but not to challenge its capacity to adapt to meet stakeholder needs.	Leaders primarily use norm-referenced test data to sort, select, and track students into programs. Improvement for all groups is the focus rather than closing data-informed gaps. Leaders believe that standardized test scores present an objective picture of the range of ability and the inevitable performance "curve" of diverse students.	Leaders may use/share data to highlight disproportionate outcomes and access to services. If they do, leaders may limit focus to one underperforming group over others or direct efforts at raising test scores without necessarily removing barriers to student learning.	Leaders use/share multiple sources of data that clarify disproportionate patterns over time for demographic groups. Leaders examine not only achievement data but also access and opportunity data to close gaps sooner rather than later when disparities show up in test score data.	Leaders share data with other organizations to build understanding about cross-organizational effectiveness in meeting underserved stakeholders' needs. From this, leaders forge a cross-agency vision and commitment to sharing resources to build organizations that change people and their capacity to structure society for socially just ends.
The extent to which the leader (1) helps others understand the sources of assumptions that may obscure the truth about the organization's effectiveness and	Leaders do not use data to create an understanding of the school's effectiveness with specific populations, nor do they use data to inform conversations and decisions. Prevailing assumptions and biases go unchallenged.	Leaders expect students and their parents to take advantage of existing school opportunities, which they believe are effectively meeting the learning needs of	Leaders believe and promote that there are factors that influence student performance that are beyond the purview of the school; therefore, there is only so much outcome data	Leaders respond to legal mandates to reduce disproportionality in specific programs or across the system. Often the measure of compliance is in the development of a plan or the delivery of a program or professional	Leaders challenge and encourage others to challenge policies, programs, and practices that correlate with disproportionate educational outcomes. They model and	Leaders challenge and encourage others to challenge and dismantle legal mandates within and outside of the educational system that create barriers to success. Leaders form coalitions to

(Continued)

(Continued)

ADAPTING TO DIVERSITY	CULTURAL DESTRUCTIVENESS	CULTURAL INCAPACITY	CULTURAL BLINDNESS	CULTURAL PRECOMPETENCE	CULTURAL COMPETENCE	CULTURAL PROFICIENCY
diminish personal responsibility for achieving it and (2) builds capacity to transform the organization's ability to achieve outcomes for equity and justice.		underperforming students. Leaders and staff cannot be held responsible if students and parents do not participate in or complete such programs.	for which the school can and should accept responsibility.	development but not in the reduction of the disproportionality.	encourage risk-taking and thinking outside of the box, while holding themselves and others accountable for adapting, learning about, and applying new programs, structures, and practices that show evidence on multiple measures of narrowing educational gaps.	lobby for legislation that ensures equitable access and outcomes for underserved stakeholders.
The extent to which the leader manifests and develops in others a congruence between personal identity and purpose and vocational identity and purpose (leadership integrity).	Leaders' identities and actions are disconnected from the moral purpose of school, often leading to passivity, cynicism, and unethical or unjust leadership.	Leaders' identities and actions are congruent with a deficit perspective of diverse students and a well-intended vocational purpose to remediate and assimilate them "for their own good."	Leaders' identities and actions are congruent with pedagogy for equality but not equity	Leaders' identities and actions are congruent with helping or rescuing some students but not necessarily removing barriers to their success.	Leaders' identities and actions are congruent with a pedagogy for educational equity (closing educational gaps).	Leaders' personal identities and purposes and vocational identities and purposes are integrated, one and the same, in their moral imperative for social justice.

INSTITUTIONALIZING CULTURAL KNOWLEDGE	CULTURAL DESTRUCTIVENESS	CULTURAL INCAPACITY	CULTURAL BLINDNESS	CULTURAL PRECOMPETENCE	CULTURAL COMPETENCE	CULTURAL PROFICIENCY
The extent to which the leader communicates openly, frequently, and effectively with all stakeholder groups and creates a culture of community collaboration and inclusive decision-making focused on meeting the needs of underserved students and their parents/guardians	Leaders avoid or resist communicating openly and effectively with all stakeholder groups, believing some will not understand or are not worthy or capable of understanding the goals or policies of the organization. Decisions are made to intentionally thwart or exclude some voices that would require the organization to reallocate resources for underserved stakeholders.	Leaders communicate frequently with stakeholder groups with the loudest or most influential voices. Decisions are made unilaterally or by a few top school leaders, believing they know what is best for all groups, without seeking input from the communities that will be affected most by the decisions.	Leaders provide equal opportunities to give and receive communication from all groups but do not see the need to accommodate the context, environment, nuance, or language for the needs of some stakeholder groups. Leaders comply with decisions made by state/federal agencies and a few top administrators, believing them to adequately benefit all stakeholders regardless of their cultural needs and styles.	Leaders may translate communications for some stakeholder groups but not others. Leaders may accommodate communication strategies consistently to ensure effective cross-cultural communication for some groups. Leaders may seek input from cultural affinity groups but may not do so consistently for all cultural groups. Well-intentioned leaders may extrapolate information from a few members of one cultural group and assume it applies to all members of that group.	Leaders model effective and polished oral and written communication in the languages of the community while accommodating the context of the communication to meet stakeholder needs. Leaders seek input from multiple and varied stakeholder groups even if some groups do not assert their voices or perspectives. Decisions are made that consider all stakeholders' input, but leaders are not afraid to make a decision that primarily supports underserved stakeholders.	Leaders collaborate with community organizations to develop and use cross-cultural communication strategies to solicit stakeholder input, develop goals, and take action that enhances multiorganizational credibility, trust, and effectiveness in meeting the needs of stakeholders. Leaders facilitate an understanding among all in the community that meeting the needs of the underserved contributes to the common good.

(Continued)

(Continued)

INSTITUTIONALIZING CULTURAL KNOWLEDGE	CULTURAL DESTRUCTIVENESS	CULTURAL INCAPACITY	CULTURAL BLINDNESS	CULTURAL PRECOMPETENCE	CULTURAL COMPETENCE	CULTURAL PROFICIENCY
The extent to which the leader promotes a persistent vision of education as the vehicle for closing societal gaps, makes a difference in the lives of others, and creates support networks and structures for mentoring greatness in others	Leaders use their position to acquire and assert authority, politicize education, and foment negative attitudes about some stakeholder groups in the school and community. Leaders use their authority to limit the power of others, grow their own power, distort information, and withhold resources for some groups. Leaders intimidate others to adopt and act on the leaders' political values.	Leaders use their authority to ensure that others comply with state and district policies and procedures, believing them to adequately meet the educational needs of most students. Leaders ignore or attempt to remediate students with special needs, limiting their future educational options and success. Leaders seek success by assimilating to the dominant culture's standards for school leaders and expect others to do the same.	Leaders use their position to reinforce the meritocratic nature of school, being unaware of or ignoring disproportionate opportunity gaps experienced by some students. That some students succeed is evidence that the system is fair. Leaders see themselves as enforcers and maintainers of current educational policy, not challengers of it.	Leaders may use their position to make others aware of the equity gap for one or a few specific demographic groups. Often such leaders become outspoken advocates for a specific underperforming group, using their position to reallocate resources for such groups but not necessarily taking the risk to remove systemic barriers for some or all underserved groups.	Leaders use their position to inform stakeholders about the organization's effectiveness in meeting the needs of underserved stakeholders. Such leaders facilitate an understanding that transforming the system requires changing the service paradigm from equality to equity and replacing a pedagogy for continuous improvement for all with a pedagogy for closing gaps for the underserved.	Leaders inspire and are inspiring. They use their position to influence state and federal policy and resources to level the educational and societal playing field. Their wisdom and beneficence develop moral purpose in others and empower and reward others' leadership successes. The fulfillment of contributing to the success of others grows the leaders' capacity for enduring greatness.

The questions posed in the Reflection section of this chapter will hone your readiness to start your own work. Chapter 4 provides specific case stories to further illustrate how the journey to Cultural Proficiency looks in the context of real issues faced by today's educational leaders. As you consider each case story, examine how you might have responded in a similar situation. By sharing and examining our responses to and progress in real-world situations, we expand the network of colleagues who inform this work and broaden its effectiveness. Remember that Cultural Proficiency is not a new program. Rather, it is a lens through which we can examine and understand our past, current, and future work to make system-wide changes that result in educational equity.

REFLECTION: THE CULTURAL PROFICIENCY LEADERSHIP RUBRIC

These activities can be conducted by individuals or, for maximum effectiveness, by a group of colleagues.

- Starting on the left side of the continuum (second column), read the cells of each vertical column from left to right. What overlapping values or assumptions correspond to the vertical columns? Continue this activity with each of the next vertical columns along the continuum. At what level of the continuum do you see a notable break in belief patterns? Do you think it is harder or easier to move the individual and the organization from any one level to another? Why/why not?

- Turn your attention to the first essential element: assessing cultural knowledge.

- Study the operational definitions of assessing cultural knowledge in the first two cells of the first vertical column. These two cells define the "essence" of assessing cultural knowledge.

- Next, read the examples for assessing cultural knowledge, beginning with *cultural destructiveness* and going through *Cultural Proficiency*. You will have read twelve illustrations along the continuum—six illustrations for each of the two sub-points of this essential element.

- What do you notice as you read from left to right? What questions and reactions do you have? If conducting the activity with colleagues, compare and discuss your observations and reactions.

_____

_____

_____

_____

- Finally, perform the same analysis with the remaining four essential elements: valuing diversity, managing the dynamics of difference, adapting to diversity, and institutionalizing cultural knowledge.

_____

_____

_____

_____

- How does completing this activity help you understand how to use the rubric to diagnose and formatively develop your values and behaviors and your school's/organization's policies and practices? What next steps might you take?

_____

_____

_____

_____

YOUR OWN APPLICATION

- You are now prepared to use the rubric on your own. What might you do first?

- What data inform your plan? What additional data will you seek to establish your baseline or current status quo? At what level of Cultural

Proficiency might your organization be functioning as a whole (realizing that individuals or some practices and policies may be at less or more effective levels of practice on the continuum)?

- How else might you apply what you have learned?

_____

_____

_____

_____

FOR ADDITIONAL CONSIDERATION

Uses of the Rubric. We have observed at least two uses of the rubric; one is inappropriate, and the other is appropriate, useful, and productive:

- Inappropriate use of the rubric involves hearing a colleague make a comment or seeing them display a behavior that you can locate on the left side of the rubric and informing them that you have demonstrable proof that they are exhibiting cultural destructiveness, cultural incapacity, or cultural blindness. While it may be tempting to point out such behavior, it neither leads to good relations with colleagues nor leads to change that benefits students.

- Appropriate use of the rubric begins with the same analysis as in the above illustration, but instead of making the other person the focus, your focus is on what you can do. For example, if the offending behavior is culturally destructive, you can use the rubric to examine options for what you should say or do by reading the culturally precompetent, culturally competent, and culturally proficient illustrations.

What we refer to as appropriate use of the rubric serves as an illustration of the "inside-out" approach of Cultural Proficiency.

The rubric provides formal and nonformal leaders with a template for action. It is not a stand-alone activity for school leaders, other educators, and their communities. It is an action tool to assess progress toward clearly defined goals focused on improving student achievement. Effective use of the rubric as a leverage point for change is dependent on deep-level conversations that emerge from using *all* four tools of Cultural Proficiency.

CHAPTER 4

....

CASE STORIES AS LESSONS

"Stories constitute the single most powerful weapon in a leader's arsenal."

Dr. Howard Gardner

The purpose of this chapter is to illuminate the theoretical tools of Cultural Proficiency with real-life stories. As you read the case stories, look for the ways the authors reflect their understanding and use of the tools of Cultural Proficiency to change the mindset of colleagues, staff, and community and to make decisions and take action to achieve equitable outcomes for underserved students. What levels of the Cultural Proficiency Leadership Rubric do you see enacted? And which essential elements are demonstrated or leveraged by the leaders to navigate the changes they wish to make? At the end of each case story, we have provided an opportunity for you to reflect on what occurred and add your own insights about how you would handle the situation.

Notice the subtle but important differences between the actions of the culturally competent leader and those of the culturally proficient leader. The culturally competent leader is an advocate for those whose voices are silenced, limited, or ignored by schools/organizations. The culturally competent leader helps students navigate the barriers to success. The culturally competent leader listens and observes to redress wrongs. The culturally proficient leader is an activist who often sounds the alarm, challenges the status quo, and removes the barriers to success. The culturally proficient leader is not "afraid to make some noise and get in good trouble, necessary trouble" (Lewis, 2018). How do these leaders exemplify culturally competent and culturally proficient leadership?

We wrote these case stories based on our moral imperative to correct a wrong. As you read each one, consider the following guiding questions. Then select one case story from the first three and write your reflection in the space provided, based on the leadership rubric. Consider your professional and lived experiences as you reflect on the questions below for your selected case story.

QUESTIONS FOR REFLECTION

1. Describe the moral imperative that drove the author's work in your selected case story.

2. Identify key strategies the author implemented in the case story.

3. What other strategies might have been implemented?

4. Consider the leader's role in taking risks on behalf of students in the face of obvious staff, community, or even elected official disagreement. How much risk is too much? What consequences should the leader consider?

5. Based on your professional experiences, cite similar examples of students being denied an equitable education. What risks are you personally willing to take to make a difference in students' lives?

CASE STORY ONE: CARMELLA S. FRANCO

Students Denied Opportunities to Optimize Success

Context

In 2010, I was appointed by the State Board of Education (SBE) to serve as the state trustee of a school district in Monterey County, California. The SBE had taken the powers away from this district and its board of education due to failure to meet the educational needs of English learners. So egregious were the data, this was the first and only time the state had executed this option. The district was 95 percent Hispanic, and many students came from migrant families. The rates at which English-learner students were being reclassified to English were abysmal. I made a highly controversial decision to change the existing practice whereby Spanish-speaking students were expected to transition to English-proficient and English-only instruction by the end of third grade. That practice assumed that students would make a smooth transition from third-grade Spanish proficiency to third-grade English proficiency. I was appalled by the longitudinal data that showed that students who had begun in the district as non-English-speaking kindergartners and were now in eleventh grade were still categorized as English learners and non-proficient in English. That was after eleven years in the system! Armed with those data, I enacted an initiative to ensure that students were afforded the opportunity to learn English. The initiative was laid out in four semesters for kindergarten through first grade, with the students beginning as non-English speakers and progressing to English-only instruction by the end of first grade.

Complexity

The teachers, with the exception of a handful, were excited to embark on the journey of ensuring that students transitioned from Spanish to English instruction by the end of first grade. Parents thanked me for "allowing their children to learn English in school." The curriculum was developed and unveiled for immediate implementation. I was amazed by the progress I witnessed as I visited classrooms. I saw chart paper with the students' work and stories written in English and listened to the students responding in English during their lessons. At the end of the first year of implementation, the state California English Language Development Test (CELDT) results showed that students had excelled, most having met the requirements for reclassification to English proficient on this state assessment test. Despite this, a group of twenty or thirty district and community members, some not associated with the district, spoke against the initiative at most board meetings. They argued that the original bilingual instructional program for kindergarten and first grade should be restored to replace the initiative, the reason being: *"This is the way we have always done it."* On a daily basis I also dealt with district board and interim leadership who attempted to undermine my actions, but because of my firm belief in the rights of children to a quality education, the published efficacy of the program being implemented, and my high expectations for both students and staff to be successful with the new initiative, I did not back down, give in, or apologize.

More Complexities

Busloads of parents—who we later discovered were paid—traveling to Sacramento to speak against the initiative at SBE meetings was a monthly event. SBE members were pressured by myriad groups, including California legislators, who wanted power returned to the district's previous board members, who now served in a strictly advisory role. The issue of students not being afforded the opportunity to learn English and not being successful in society was not on their front burner, as their interests were solely adult-issue driven. I was summoned to meet individually with local legislators. I was told by one elected official that there were people who wanted to "take me out." I had acid poured on my car, and I never had it removed. I drove into the district parking lot every day with that burn mark on my car to show that I was not leaving. I could have had hired security but chose not to during my twenty-five months in the district as state trustee. My focus was on improving learning for a group of students whose educational needs had been ignored for too long.

Relevance

Advocating for this particular implementation was not an easy decision for me as a Latina, former bilingual teacher, and Title VII director. I was even accused of being anti-bilingual education. That was a ridiculous accusation. My decision was not about bilingual versus monolingual English instruction. It was about quality instruction that met the language readiness and learning needs of this group of students.

From the day I decided to implement the Learning English initiative, I never took the blinders off. My mission was to keep politics out of the classroom and to ensure that students were being provided with the instruction they needed to be successful. If we'd had the luxury of offering intensive professional development and other resources to impact the quality of instruction over time, I might have taken a different route. However, there was no time to do that. Each day that passed, more and more underserved students were receiving less and less of what they needed. In spite of the controversy and the negative reaction of some in the school community, my decision and leadership were supported by the SBE and its president, for which I am grateful to this day and which helped me stay the course. The bilingual program in grades two and three continued in the district, and model dual-language programs were being studied for implementation during and after my tenure. The struggle was worth it.

Reflections

This is the first time I have written in any detail about those twenty-five months as the state-appointed trustee of this district. That span of time was difficult, sometimes painful, due to the way my intentions were distorted, and I was personally vilified. But this was also a time of reaping the benefits and rewards of risk-taking that resulted in positive outcomes. At the end of the second year of implementation of the new instructional program, this district was the only one in Monterey County to show two consecutive years of growth on the CELDT. Other districts in the county showed growth the first or second year, but none showed it for two consecutive years. Aside from the professional and academic rewards, I have a vision in my mind of little kindergartners and first graders happily chattering away in English, in addition to their home language. I recall the day in my second year as state trustee when a crowd of parents gathered at the district one morning to greet me. Not knowing what the issue was, I had them escorted to the boardroom, where I braced myself for their anticipated concern. One of the parents, all of whom spoke only Spanish and the majority of whom were migrant workers, came up to the front of the boardroom and took my hand. She said the parents wanted to thank me for seeing that their children learned English. Her words: "Thank you, Dr. Franco. You see that our children learn English in school, and we will teach them Spanish at home." I thought, *I have realized what I came here to do.* Would I do it again? Absolutely, yes, *for the children.*

QUESTIONS FOR REFLECTION

- Describe the moral imperative that drove the author's work in this case story.

_____

_____

_____

_____

- Identify key strategies the author implemented in the case story.

_____

_____

_____

_____

- What other strategies might have been implemented?

_____

_____

_____

_____

(Continued)

(Continued)

- Consider the leader's role in taking risks on behalf of students in the face of obvious staff, community, or even elected official disagreement. How much risk is too much? What consequences should the leader consider?

  _____

  _____

  _____

  _____

- Based on your professional experiences, cite similar examples of students being denied an equitable education. What risks are you personally willing to take to make a difference in students' lives?

  _____

  _____

  _____

  _____

CASE STORY TWO: MARIA G. OTT

District of Choice

Context

Our leadership journey as educators is about learning to know who we are, what we value, and how we can leave a meaningful legacy for children, families, and communities. I stopped many times on my leadership journey to check for clarity and purpose in my work. Was I making a difference that mattered? One important stop on my journey was District of Choice legislation. I share this story as an example of how someone who believes deeply in parental choice could end up fighting against it in her role as superintendent of a medium-sized school district. As background, my beliefs about choice are rooted in my experiences as a child and in the influence of my parents. My parents had limited means and limited schooling, but they were convinced that my two brothers and sister and I would have a better chance if we went to Catholic schools. They could barely afford the tuition; my father saved tips from his work as a barber, and my mother saved money from cleaning houses. Their sacrifices shaped my belief that parents know what they want and what is best for their children. So how does an educator influenced by this experience find herself as the poster child for a fight against choice?

The story begins when I was hired by the board of education of a respected medium-sized district in Los Angeles County. During the interview, the board members stressed that they needed a leader who could address declining enrollment in their district. Declining enrollment strips a district of its ability to maintain services and enrich the educational experiences of its students. The loss of students and resources was undermining what the district valued for its students. My district was diverse, representing a majority of Latinx, Asian, Filipino, and Black students. White students made up less than 10 percent of the enrollment. While the board members talked about their need for a leader who could understand and address the decline, I contemplated how a public relations campaign would stop the loss of students. What I saw was a highly regarded suburban district that needed better public relations. I completely missed the facts of the situation by looking at the problem on the surface and failed to grasp the magnitude and complexity. This was an important leadership lesson, as it taught me not to accept obvious solutions.

I came to the district after five years in the Los Angeles Unified School District (LAUSD) as the senior deputy superintendent to Roy Romer, the former governor of Colorado and a nationally respected political influencer. I worked alongside Roy Romer to address public confidence in the LAUSD schools. Naively, I thought I could bring the political skills gained from working within the complex LAUSD environment to turn around public confidence in my new district. I understood the significance of declining enrollment and its impact on students and their community. My lack of information led me to misinterpret how to approach the challenge. Since my district was considered one of the success stories in serving diverse students and valuing educational innovation, it seemed intuitive that just getting that message out consistently would turn the tide.

My first effort focused on a "Grow Where You Are Planted" campaign. A public relations expert was hired to distribute information about the district's successes and to push out positive stories from school sites to parents and the larger community. Although a feel-good approach, the campaign did little to stop the loss of students.

I failed to understand that my new district was experiencing enrollment decline due to District of Choice legislation passed by the California Legislature in 1993 as a way to promote parental choice. The legislation allowed students to transfer to districts that had, by resolution of the school board, declared themselves Districts of Choice. The program allowed a district to accept students without notifying the home district. Failure to share data was the main reason that my district did not understand the full story behind the decline in enrollment. The traditional approvals used for the transfer of students between school districts did not apply, and more than 1,200 students from my district had been enrolled to fill vacant seats in the neighboring district. Data were not required to be shared with the district of residence, the county office of education, or the state department of education. In addition, during the early years of District of Choice implementation, no oversight was in place to ensure that a participating district followed the language within the legislation.

My story of awakening started with educating myself on the law and understanding what had occurred between my district and the neighboring district. Although the message was about choice, the reality was that students were being sorted, and those who participated were more advantaged and less diverse than students in the district they were leaving.

Complexity

Examining the complexity of the problem and its impact on my district, I was outraged! I was angry to find that the provisions in the legislation were ignored; for example, in the original version of the legislation, a participating district that offered home-to-school transportation was required to offer this to students accepted under the District of Choice. I viewed this as an opportunity for accepted students to be treated to the same benefits as resident students. However, offering transportation was clearly a disincentive for participating districts, as the costs would counterbalance the revenue benefits the students would bring to their new district. So such a resource was not offered. In addition, a district participating in the District of Choice program was required to accept English learners, special-needs students, and low-income students, but our neighboring district did not accept such students as they would increase its costs. Was this the choice that was envisioned by those who wrote the policy? Or was this a way to fill seats without additional effort or cost on the part of the District of Choice?

Choice is one of the most debated issues facing public education across the nation. Starting with the work of economist Milton Friedman, who promoted choice options as a way to improve school performance through competition, considerable debate around the benefits of choice has fueled the larger debate that includes charters, vouchers, and public-funded tuition scholarships. As an educator, I am deeply committed to offering options that benefit students' opportunities for academic success. My own experience as a child whose parents wanted something more for me taught me that choice should be an option for parents. However, was this version of choice the vision that policymakers and the public desired and deserved?

What I witnessed went to the core of the national debate about choice. While choice sounds appealing, when implemented in ways that give already advantaged students more opportunities, it results in negative impacts on other students, primarily students of color and socioeconomically disadvantaged students. My outrage led me to conclude that leaders need to be aware. They need to understand choice policies and challenge those that are suspect in their goals and outcomes. They need to ask if choice policies further divide those *with* and those *without* privilege. In a society that seeks to advance the American dream for all, what are the right choice policies, and which are policies that need to be challenged and changed? That became my work: to question, challenge, confront, and advocate for change.

I became the face of the District of Choice debate in California, and my advocacy work would change how I was viewed as a leader and disrupter of the status quo. I worked with elected leaders to make changes to the law that would add a level of accountability and prevent its misuse in ways that harmed students due to unfair implementation.

Data were needed to challenge the unfair implementation of District of Choice. The data were not available in any database accessible to the public. I knew that data were recorded by the District of Choice for internal record-keeping, but when asked to share the data, the district's answer was no. Responses to requests for information were answered with a solid "not available." It was necessary to create the database, one student at a time, by examining records available in my district for former students and students who were expected but never enrolled. Principals of schools within my district that were high performing and not designated as Title I were helpful, as these principals were most aware of families that enrolled in District of Choice. These schools were most impacted by the loss of students and shared my sense of urgency. Some of their information came from personal knowledge, and some was shared with them by families who resented the exodus of students. The data collected confirmed that students who were English learners, had special needs, and/or were eligible for free and reduced meals were not the students recruited to participate in District of Choice. As overall enrollment declined by more than 1,200 students, the percentage of students in my district needing special support increased. It was evident that the students who were selected for District of Choice were students without the need for additional educational supports. It was a simple mathematical fact: as overall enrollment declined, the proportion of students with educational-support needs increased in my district. The students leaving my district did not have these needs; they were students who already had the resources and opportunities to be successful. Delving into the facts of District of Choice confirmed my interpretation of what occurred and increased my outrage. This was not the choice I valued as a way to offer opportunities to students living in poverty or lacking the experiences needed to enter school on equal footing with their more advantaged peers. How had this policy been allowed to go so far without anyone realizing the egregious practices hidden from public view under the choice label?

I learned that the policy adopted by the legislature in California used language that, on the surface, sounded like it would give educational options to students and their parents who were in situations that were not meeting their academic needs. In practice, it sorted students by their backgrounds, language abilities, and economic circumstances. The legislation came about as an alternative to vouchers, and some legislators actually believed that this legislation would open the doors for students in underperforming schools and from poverty backgrounds to attend schools with higher performance and more advantages. In practice, it exacerbated inequality.

My district was the victim of this deceit in the early days of the legislation. What was said in the language of District of Choice looked nothing like the practice. Our neighboring school district had very different demographics. They had fewer students of color from diverse backgrounds, fewer English learners, and fewer special-needs students, and they were in serious enrollment decline. This neighboring district declared itself an early adopter of this legislation, allowing the district to fill its empty seats with students it selected, primarily from the adjacent areas located in my district. The selected students matched the profile of the district's existing students as evidenced by the socioeconomic indicators for the neighboring district not changing and its enrollment remaining stable during its District of Choice participation. However, in my district, enrollment was declining and students living in poverty increased as a proportion of entire enrollment. My district became less diverse and increased its percentage of English learners and students living below the poverty line.

The implementation of this legislation in my district was not about equity. It was about benefiting a district that needed enrollment to thrive fiscally but wanted that enrollment to match its resident population, which was predominantly white, Asian, and middle-class. I experienced anger and repulsion in realizing that public policy was being used to reinforce the status quo, and no one seemed to care at the statehouse. Words like *anger* and *repulsion* are not typical for my leadership vocabulary, but this is exactly what I felt. District of Choice was harming students whom I was charged to protect and defend from poorly implemented public policies.

Relevance

What went wrong? In the early years of the policy, there was no provision for oversight. No one was required to keep a record or report on the impact of the policy. The handful of districts that participated were able to operate without publishing any outcome data. Most were in rural areas with issues different from those faced by my district. So although the language of the policy had certain requirements, such as offering home-to-school transportation for accepted students, there was no oversight to determine if this was actually occurring. Having a policy or a resource that intends to help underperforming students but does not provide them realistic access to the resource is one indicator that the policy is flawed. This is a way that systems hide behind good intentions that have negative results for the very students the policy was designed to help. This approach is harmful to students who should be protected by well-designed and well-implemented educational policies.

Creating a destructive narrative: District of Choice created a narrative that children attending certain schools in my district were attending schools that were less desirable and that enrolling in the neighboring district would be an advantage. The students who departed to the neighboring district were largely not low-income or English learners and did not need special education services, so the implementation of the policy clearly augmented the enrollment of a district experiencing declining enrollment while not imposing the burden of any additional financial expectations or consequences. On the other hand, my district needed to continue to reduce services as a result of the loss of students and loss of revenue. Because the percentage of students in my district remained stable in terms of low-income students, English learners, and special-needs students, the proportion of these special populations increased. It was necessary to reduce my district's budget each year to accommodate the loss of students while experiencing a continued need to increase special support services with fewer resources to meet this responsibility. Is this narrative that pits one district against another helpful? Or is this a narrative to justify perpetuating privilege for those who already have it? Is this a narrative that fulfills the American dream for students who rely on effective public policy to have access to academic and societal success? I think it is not!

On a personal level, I could see the value of choice options that benefit students who have disadvantages. Unfortunately, the District of Choice legislation did not provide opportunities for students who were poor, English learners, or diagnosed with special needs to have those choices. These special learners were not the students selected for the District of Choice. On the other side of this equation, when students who are already doing well in their home district are selected to attend schools in a neighboring district with students who have similar demographics, it appears that "choice" has a new definition. My experiences as a superintendent leading the district that was most impacted by District of Choice legislation taught me that this was instead a well-intentioned but misused and contrived attempt to maintain the relentless advance of meritocracy in schools and other societal institutions. While this may have appeared to be a subtle outcome to some citizens, it seemed obvious to me. Some stakeholders were offered a preference; others were not even in the game. The status quo remained. Those whom we allow to choose will choose the best for themselves, leaving no choice for the others.

The role of legislators: When District of Choice legislation came up for renewal, I hoped it would be allowed to sunset as other choice options were available to parents, including charter schools and laws allowing parental authority to change the management of failing schools. Discussing the flaws in District of Choice legislation with the senator who represented a large portion of my district, I found him both misinformed and unsympathetic to the issues impacting my district.

The fact that District of Choice data were not shared with the community was a reason to question how a school district could take more than 1,200 students from another district without sharing that information with the public. Clearly, this happened due to the failure of elected officials to provide a feedback loop for this public policy. The lack of students eligible for free and reduced lunch accepted by the neighboring district should have raised questions, but it did not until I arrived as superintendent and put a spotlight on what was going on in the name of equal opportunity for disadvantaged students. The disadvantaged students were the ones left behind.

I will never forget my conversations with the senator when he sponsored the extension of the legislation before it was going to sunset. He informed me that District of Choice was providing an avenue for students in failing schools to attend high-performing schools in their neighboring district.

When I shared the data indicating that the percentage of students in poverty in my district was climbing in exact proportion to the loss of students to District of Choice, he still did not understand. I said, "The students leaving are privileged. This legislation violates everything the legislature says you value and support."

After two missed opportunities to take District of Choice off the legislative books, I found a sympathetic elected official in a state assembly member who had the wisdom to understand the policy issues and was open to discussing changes needed to ensure equity and fairness in District of Choice. His understanding of the key issues helped him formulate the arguments used to change the legislation. The new language provided a provision that capped the number of students a district could lose under District of Choice. The changes in the law led to an eventual showdown in the courts when my district sued to enforce the new legislative language. The success of the court action closed the door to District of Choice for my district. Unfortunately, other districts became targets, and the challenges continue to this day.

Reflections

When a district is experiencing declining enrollment, leaders must consider the impact of any efforts designed to fill vacant seats at the cost of a colleague district. We must ask, who are the students we intend to serve? And we must further ask which students are better served as a result of the implementation of the policy. Astute leaders must demand data and challenge outcomes that do not align with intentions. For any policy that includes resource allocation, reallocation, or decisions that promise to help one population over another, data must be demanded and examined! Data are key for holding decision-makers accountable and protecting the good of vulnerable student populations.

If a district opens its doors to students outside of its boundary, leaders should consider welcoming the least-advantaged students and demonstrate that choice is an opportunity to showcase the choice district's expertise in improving outcomes for low-income students, English learners, and special-needs students. That would show the importance of advancing the public good and helping realize the American dream for all students. It is incumbent on educational leaders as well as elected officials to protect the public good, which includes protecting the good of special groups.

QUESTIONS FOR REFLECTION

- Describe the moral imperative that drove the author's work in this case story.

  _____

  _____

  _____

  _____

- Identify key strategies the author implemented in the case story.

  _____

  _____

  _____

  _____

- What other strategies might have been implemented?

  _____

  _____

  _____

  _____

- Consider the leader's role in taking risks on behalf of students in the face of obvious staff, community, or even elected official disagreement. How much risk is too much? What consequences should the leader consider?

  _____

  _____

  _____

  _____

- Based on your professional experiences, cite similar examples of students being denied an equitable education. What risks are you personally willing to take to make a difference in students' lives?

_____

_____

_____

_____

CASE STORY THREE: DARLINE P. ROBLES

Importance of Data and Informed Decision-Making

Context

In 1995 I began my eight-year tenure as superintendent in a new school district. When I was hired, I was the first woman and person of color to lead the district. In fact, I was hired, to a great extent, because of who I was and my professional experience. The board of education was impressed specifically with the academic achievement of the students in my previous district. The board was concerned that the changing demographics in the district, which were similar to those in my previous district, could impact the district's academic reputation. The board did not want their district to become an urban school district that did not reflect the high academic standards they held for all their students.

When I was hired, the board asked me to improve the academic achievement of specific students, recent immigrants, English-language learners, and ethnic and racially identified students. As one board member mentioned, the fact that I had specific professional experiences was a plus, but just as important, as a Latina, I would bring my personal perspective to the work.

I knew going into the position that my presence would be supported by various communities representing the many diverse cultural groups in the district and also criticized by other communities. Despite the mixed reception, I knew I would serve as a necessary role model and this would provide me the opportunity to share my cultural identity with the majority population. Furthermore, I would serve as an example to the broader community that students from minoritized communities can and will be successful and can be leaders of large, complex organizations.

My first goal was to meet with community leaders. Over the first two months, I intentionally reached out to community organizations, churches, and non-profits working with diverse community members, who, prior to my arrival, had little voice at the district level and/or school level. I also reached out to all school parent organizations, teacher and administrator groups, business leaders, higher education leaders, and service clubs. I worked diligently to attend all community events, listening to community concerns so I was visible and approachable. My presence provided me the opportunity to hear from multiple voices and perspectives. This laid the groundwork for me to share with my board that the work we would begin would not be easy, as we now had to approach it all with an equity mindset. The board and I attended sessions on equity, both at the district and national level, so we all had a similar language and understanding of what it was going to take to make the changes necessary so students who were not achieving would be at the center of our work. We began by disaggregating data from multiple sources. We disaggregated it by racial/ethnic groups, economic status, years in the district, course-taking patterns, transiency within the district, dropout status, and disciplinary referrals and suspensions, just to name a few.

One concern that was expressed often was the insufficient representation of the diversity of the community in leadership roles at the district and school-site level, including among teachers. The school district was nationally known for its site-based decision-making process that included site decision-making on budgets and hiring. Yet there were no requirements or guidelines for hiring appropriate staff for this community, nor was there any accountability for the hiring decisions made by the schools. There was no expectation that the school would interview diverse candidates. I discussed this with the board, as the board, not school committees, is ultimately responsible for all hires. Part of the problem was that school-level committees, heavily invested in local site-based decision-making, determined who would be on the selection and hiring committees. I discussed specific changes with the board of education, which accepted my recommendations. First, the school committees had to have representation from various constituent groups, not only from the parent-teacher association but also from diverse communities that reflected the demographics of the school. The expectation that members of the selection committee had to recruit parents from racial/ethnic groups in their community was, at first, not fully embraced but over time was accepted. In addition, the committee had to send me at least two to three finalists to interview, and I would select the finalist to recommend to the board for the position. This was a major change and was not readily accepted, as school committees in the past had made the final selection. I often reminded community members and the board that we hire for the school district, not just for a specific school. The most important change was ensuring that "minoritized" community members were represented in the selection process in various ways at the school-site and district level.

A similar process was used for the selection of district-level administrators. Over the eight years, I was able to hire more women, people of color, and bilingual administrators. Not only were the faces visibly diverse, but also new ideas and perspectives were being invited and shared where they had been discouraged or considered of low precedence in the past.

Complexity

The district had been involved in site-based decision-making for more than twenty years, and all the schools were accustomed to complete autonomy, but often without accountability. Dominant voices and visible communities were able to push their agendas over the specific needs of students who were most in need, according to our data. The new administrator selection process played an important role in the changes districts were obligated to make with new federal requirements under No Child Left Behind (NCLB).

The new voices from previously unheard communities were instrumental in the district's making substantial changes to how it collected academic data (even before NCLB). Parents of students who were not succeeding academically reflected the changing demographics and voiced their concerns about their children. The analysis of the academic data provided the board and me with the necessary information to make long-term changes that narrowed the gap in academic achievement in the district within three years. In addition, we began to de-track students. When we analyzed the data on course-taking patterns, we noticed many of our English learners were in "office practice" classes or three to four ESL classes, with very few taking classes required to graduate. We began to eliminate "office practice" classes and other low-status classes and offered students access to courses required for high school graduation, along with language assistance to support our English learners, and we opened AP courses without requiring a teacher recommendation.

Alignment with a new selection process, new academic requirements, increased opportunity for underserved students, analysis of academic data across different matrices, and adjustments to site-based decision-making with accountability measures all moved the district forward in narrowing the academic gap for students who lived in low-income communities,

English learners, and racially and ethnically diverse students. The reallocation of resources or the expectation that school resources were to be targeted to improve educational outcomes for all, especially those students who had been underserved in the past, made a difference within three years. Gaps were narrowing and closing. One highlight I recall was during a board meeting where we were sharing our academic data, as we did quarterly throughout the school year. Our English learners scored as high as our English-only students at all grade levels. The board member seated next to me commented, "Now, Darline, I understand what you mean by equity; all students can learn." This "aha" came about only through six years of intensive training on Cultural Proficiency for all school employees, holding schools accountable to demonstrate growth through an annual academic plan for their schools, and being transparent with data that highlighted closing gaps over improvement for all.

Moving toward Cultural Proficiency requires all stakeholders, and specifically leaders, to understand how to value and embrace their own and others' cultures but also to leverage cultural assets for better communication, relationships, and learning. Leaders must hold themselves accountable for specific goals, often informed by the cultural learning needs of students. Without a mindset for equity over equality, data-informed practices, and holding everyone accountable across the system, the academic gaps will continue to exist within minoritized communities. After eight years of consistent focus on Cultural Proficiency, data analysis, and holding ourselves accountable for student outcomes, high expectations and results became the norm.

As superintendent, I focused my performance goals on student achievement and community involvement. My performance goals were then translated to goals for cabinet members, their direct reports, and school-site principals. Everyone knew we had to be transparent in sharing the data and holding ourselves accountable for closing gaps. But I knew it first and foremost. I held myself as accountable as I did everyone else. For these changes to work across the system, I had to lead the charge and be as accountable to the outcomes as I expected everyone else to be.

Relevance

Within the current political environment, where it is the good of the individual over the good of many, the lessons from my tenure in the district indicate that there must be a moral imperative to our work for the sake of education and the communities we serve. The alignment of the work requires us to ensure that educational equity and societal justice remain close partners.

But before coherence between schools and communities, there must be a district-wide imperative for closing equity gaps. Education or society is not democratic if the same students lag behind year after year. We must care about and ensure that everyone succeeds, especially those who our data show have been underserved in the past. It was often cited in the district that one could not be happy or proud of one's own school's accomplishments if students across the city were struggling. We learned to care for each other, learn from each other, celebrate each other's success, and work together to help everyone succeed.

As systems leaders, we must value and embrace diversity as a strength. A leader must model the strength of diversity through action and expectations. Seeing a leader of color willing to engage in dialogue about the importance of valuing their identity and expecting the same from others can set the stage for all employees in the system to respect the cultural identities of those they serve.

The expectation that leaders must hold themselves and others accountable for the success of students who have not been served well by the system is nonnegotiable. We must have high expectations for the students we serve today and for ourselves. We must be accountable for closing the academic and opportunity gaps.

To close gaps, leaders must be willing to be transparent about the data, both for academic outcomes and for opportunities we offer our students. Data are used to inform constituents about the status quo. Data also can help justify the reallocation of resources, which is often an unpopular but necessary decision. Data help tell our story and prioritize changes and next steps. Even when the data might be hard to accept, they are the first resource we must use to raise the level of concern for those inside and outside of the system. Sharing these data in the district was at the heart of our transformation. Once our data were public, there was no turning back. We had to move forward.

To move forward, we confronted ugly truths about who was not well served by the system. This knowledge set the stage for making necessary system changes that required ongoing training on Cultural Proficiency throughout my tenure in the district. It also required all of us to act with an equity mindset. We continued to share academic and opportunity data on a quarterly basis at board meetings and at public community meetings. Late in my tenure, a board member mentioned to me that one of her community members commented to her that they were tired of hearing me say "equity." I responded respectfully, "If that community member could give me another word that means the same, I would be happy to use it, but until then, I will use 'equity.'" The board member understood, as did her community members, that we were focused on closing the gap for students who were not being served well and also focused on holding ourselves accountable to meet the academic goal of the district—that *all* students will achieve academic excellence.

Knowing and respecting the community you serve is a critical element of Cultural Proficiency. But most of all, we held ourselves accountable for knowing who all our students were, knowing what their needs were, and doing whatever it took to meet those needs. It was not easy, but it was worth the journey.

Reflections

The journey to move the district to an equity mindset was not without its issues or conflicts. But the conflicts helped bring out the "elephant in the room." Many in the district were quite uncomfortable with the data and our conversations, which I noticed from people talking *around* the issues and proposing ideas that would keep everyone in a comfortable place. The important work of Cultural Proficiency often makes people *uncomfortable*. And that is okay, *maybe even necessary,* if it reveals the truth about dirty little secrets we cover up, helps people let go of deficit beliefs they have about some children and their parents, and helps people understand the role they play in perpetuating the status quo in a meritocracy, which does not serve some children well. The students and community members who were served well by the system did not want changes and were often not willing to understand why changes were needed. Communicating the "why" of our work was essential. The message I and others used consistently was, "A rising tide lifts all boats." When we work to reduce disparities, all of us win and no one loses. This message was demonstrated by concrete evidence we shared. The academic and opportunity data clearly showed that more students were succeeding, and those who were always succeeding continued to do so. No, we did not teach to the middle; we focused on moving everyone to high standards and closing gaps. The journey toward equity-minded decision-making was worth every step we took for eight years.

QUESTIONS FOR REFLECTION

- Describe the moral imperative that drove the author's work in this case story.

_____

_____

_____

_____

- Identify key strategies the author implemented in the case story.

_____

_____

_____

_____

- What other strategies might have been implemented?

_____

_____

_____

_____

- Consider the leader's role in taking risks on behalf of students in the face of obvious staff, community, or even elected official disagreement? How much risk is too much? What consequences should the leader consider?

_____

_____

_____

_____

(Continued)

(Continued)

- Based on your professional experiences, cite similar examples of students being denied an equitable education. What risks are you personally willing to take to make a difference in students' lives?

_____

_____

_____

_____

CASE STORY FOR APPLICATION

After reading the first three case stories, read the fourth one, review the Cultural Proficiency Leadership Rubric and become familiar with the language and the continuum, and complete a brief analysis of this case using the space below the case story. Identify a cell and begin your analysis across the leadership rubric.

In the previous case stories, we provided the analyses of the scenarios (see the Appendix). We explained where and why we would locate actions and decisions along the leadership rubric (*destructive* to *proficient*). We did this for both the ineffective practices and for the more effective decisions and actions made by the leader. In addition, we analyzed the extent to which the standards of behavior within the five essential elements of Cultural Proficiency were used (or not used) by constituents, decision-makers, staff, and leaders. The five essential elements are assessing cultural knowledge, valuing diversity, managing the dynamics of difference, adapting to diversity, and institutionalizing cultural knowledge for responsive transformation.

Now it is your turn to apply what you have learned about Cultural Proficiency to this final case story. Read the case story for application, then conduct your own analysis by answering the questions at the end. This can be done individually or with colleagues to solicit multiple perspectives and enrich discussion. Note that there is not necessarily one best answer or response. In fact, we challenge you to try to justify multiple responses to the same question.

How One Superintendent Used Data to Drive Change

Context

The district where I was superintendent for eight years was nationally known for its site-based decision-making process for many years prior to my arrival as superintendent. It was a process I was familiar with and supported, but one of the major elements of the process that I found missing was accountability. Who was accountable for the decisions being made, the impact of the site decision on other parts of the system, and, more important, the impact on students and families?

As part of my initial work as superintendent, I began to look at academic data from multiple sources. The district had a wealth of data by school and by student demographics going back several years. When I asked to see the data, the staff person who had collected the data over time was very happy to share. That was when I found out no one at the district level had analyzed the data or thought of analyzing the data for each school. In fact, it seemed that no one prior to me had even asked to see the data.

One interesting recollection is when I reviewed the reading and math data for elementary schools and noted that even in high-performing schools there were students not reading at grade level. I met with each principal and asked this question: "Of what you control, what can you do to improve the reading levels of the students in your school who are not reading at grade level?" The most common responses started with, "Well, if parents . . ." or "If students. . . ." I would stop them and again ask what they could do, not what others could do. It would take time for them to consider this question, and more time for them to provide a response. One principal shared that if I would look at the data for students who had been in his school since kindergarten and stayed until the end of sixth grade, I would see that those students did well; so if all students remained at the school, all students would be reading at grade level. He went on to tell me that the transiency rate at the school was in the 80th percentile, and currently he had only about six students in his sixth-grade class who had been at the school since kindergarten. Now, I had moved to five schools by the fourth grade, so I understood transiency as a student, but this was not a reason to expect students not to be able to read at grade level.

This conversation led me to take a closer look into student mobility at the elementary level. At first, principals misinterpreted the data trend as the normal transfer of students to and from other districts. The data indicated otherwise. More than 70 percent of the student mobility was within the district.

As I was analyzing the data at the elementary level, the district was also engaged in reviewing its high school dropout data. My director of student services and her team were determined to find all the students and interview them. This was a herculean effort, but she and her staff did it. What we found was that students would move out of a high school attendance area and enroll in another high school in the district and then drop out. They dropped out because they could not keep up with the work. Either the classes were not similar to their other high school courses, or the teachers were farther into the material than their previous teacher, or the content was a repeat of what they had already learned. The misarticulation of curriculum from school to school, within the same district, had become a barrier to student learning and led to many students dropping out of school completely. For both the elementary and high school student experience, families moved for a variety of reasons, but the most prevalent reason was the affordability of housing. Families could not afford the rent increase, or lost employment and had to move in with family members, or became homeless.

Complexity

Understanding the issues for both elementary and high school required asking several specific questions about how programmatic issues, including curriculum alignment and articulation, were decided at the school level, and the extent to which those making the decisions knew or were concerned about how their decisions were impacting students across the district.

At the elementary level, site-based decision-making had moved to individual teacher decision-making. The district did not require schools to adopt the same curriculum across grade levels or to ensure that selected programs were articulated within grade levels. For example, within the same district, a first-grade teacher could choose to use a "whole language approach" to reading, while another first-grade teacher could choose to teach reading through phonics. A second-grade teacher could use a basal reader or any other teaching method. These individual decisions, seemingly made according to teacher preference, could occur and were occurring at any given elementary school in the district. The misalignment and misarticulation of teaching methods may not have harmed students who entered kindergarten already reading, as many in our district who lived in affluent areas did. But for students who were recent immigrants, English learners, or transient students, this was problematic. And even in our affluent areas, the misalignment was an issue for struggling readers and special-needs students.

That no one at the school level was accountable for these decisions called for an urgent resolution. I shared my concerns with the principals and the board. It was clear they did not know that a majority of the student mobility was within the district and in schools very close to each other. There were many heated discussions on what to do while still maintaining site-based decision-making at the school level. My response, with board agreement, was that we would still honor site-based decision-making but with certain parameters, not simply teacher preference. Decisions would have to be considered from the standpoint of what was best for the students, always being conscious of which students would be most impacted by curriculum misalignment and misarticulation. Highly transient students who were disproportionately affected were Latinx, Samoan, Indigenous (Navajo Nation), recent immigrants, and refugees.

It was decided that the district would provide several K–3 reading programs, which all sites could review to select one program. The same applied to grades four and five. A few teachers and site administrators were not happy, but I was able to work with the local teachers association, who understood and supported the importance of a better-articulated curriculum to meet the needs of a diverse student population.

Over time, the decision made an impact across the district. Reading proficiency improved, and we did close the gaps for some groups. I recall the interaction I had with one student while visiting an elementary school to celebrate the reading achievements there. When I entered the classroom, I was introduced by the teacher as the superintendent. I asked the fourth-grade class if anyone had any idea what I did. A few students said I inspected the schools, making sure everything worked well, and then one young boy said, "You take care of super people." I then asked him who were the super people, and he quickly responded, "Us!" Yes, he was right; my job is to take care of all the super people in my district.

For the high school level, it was again important to ask the right questions, including asking teachers and administrators to consider how their decisions impacted students across the district. We had three comprehensive high schools and one continuation high school. The three high schools each had a unique reputation and were all dearly loved by the students, teachers, and alumni. Over time, through site-based decision-making, each school selected its own academic calendar. One school was on the semester calendar, another on the quarter calendar, and the other on a trimester calendar. At first, and for many years, this may not have been a problem. But over time and as the student and community demographics changed, the misaligned academic calendars across the district increased the dropout rate to close to 12 percent. When analyzing the mobility rate of high school students within the district and the impact this had on students of color and students from low-income communities, it became clear that site-based decisions regarding school-specific academic calendars could not continue.

When I shared the data with the board and the high school principals, there was, of course, pushback. There was a lot of controversy, and many dug in their heels and would not even consider a possible change. On the board was a high school teacher who worked in another district, and he was very vocal in his support for one common academic calendar. As he often stated, "Structures don't teach; we teach." During the many board discussions, the high schools were asked to provide data and rationales for their unique calendars and to address how their unique calendars would accommodate student mobility.

Each school had an opportunity to state its case. In reality, there were no clear data that demonstrated one academic calendar worked better for students, though it was clear that some calendars worked better for some teachers. The point the schools made over and over again was that this was a site decision and the board and superintendent were violating the spirit of site-based decision-making by imposing strictures or requirements. I often reminded the board and others that the decisions made at the site had to consider the impact on other sites in the district and the academic impact on current and future students. As expected, I heard many ugly racial comments about "those kids" and "those parents," and "Why are they here?" and "Who cares if they drop out?" It was a very intense time for the board, but ultimately they understood what it meant to lead for equity and voted to have one academic calendar.

Relevance

All of us want to have a voice in decisions that affect us. It makes sense that those closest to the problem or issue should make the decision. What is usually left out of the decision-making process, however, is the impact of the decision outside of the decision-maker's purview. Schools are microcosms of their larger communities and are impacted by the economic and social issues affecting those communities. To make decisions in isolation of the known or projected impact on current and future student populations is irresponsible leadership because such decisions can, and often do, harm the most vulnerable students.

Reflections

As I look back, I realize I was fortunate to work with a board that was willing to make decisions with an equity mindset. Because of our working together, along with the eventual cooperation of our teachers, principals, and district leaders, our academic achievement improved. Our SAT-9 scores continued to improve for several years. In 1999, twenty-four of the twenty-seven elementary schools demonstrated gains from three to twenty-eight points. In 2001, 95 percent of all schools met or exceeded their expectancy bands for SAT-9 composite scores. The student dropout rate decreased from 12 percent in 1997–1998 to 5 percent in 2000–2001. The decisions to realign district calendars and articulate curriculum within, between, and across grade levels were the right ones for *this* population. It just took awareness on the part of all staff that *these* were *our* students and it was up to everyone in *our* district to take ownership for decisions to better meet their needs.

My strong advocacy for site-based decision-making was strengthened through intensive training and expanding the demographic representation on school community councils. I also introduced an interest-based approach to decision-making and the implementation of a conflict mediation center. This required monthly meetings with all employees, parents, and community organizations that allowed constituents to listen to concerns and give input about important decisions impacting schools and the entire district. This expanded participation by the community made it harder for sites to make insular decisions and called for sites to consider community input and concerns over unjustified preferences.

REFLECTION: CASE STORIES

In the context of the case story for application, "How One Superintendent Used Data to Drive Change," answer the following questions. *(Note: there is more than one answer, depending on perspectives of various decision-makers, staff, and leaders.)*

- What were the existing conditions or the status quo that provoked the new leader's press for change? How did staff justify the current status quo?

_____

_____

_____

_____

- Considering that staff justified the existing conditions in various ways, where would you locate the district's practices, decisions, or actions along the Cultural Proficiency Leadership Rubric prior to the new leader's arrival? Explain why.

  _____

  _____

  _____

  _____

- What specific steps did the new leader take to provoke change to existing policies that she thought were creating barriers to student success? Where along the Cultural Proficiency Leadership Rubric would you locate actions on the part of the new leader? Explain why.

  _____

  _____

  _____

  _____

- How did the new leader demonstrate any or all of the five essential elements of Cultural Proficiency as she worked to change the status quo to better serve all students?

  _____

  _____

  _____

  _____

- What did you learn from this case story and/or your analysis of it that will inform your leadership practice?

  _____

  _____

  _____

  _____

CHAPTER 5

∙∙∙∙∙∙∙∙∙∙∙∙∙∙∙∙∙∙∙∙∙∙∙∙∙∙∙∙∙∙∙∙∙∙∙

PLANNING FOR EQUITY

"Every moment is an organizing opportunity, every person a potential activist, every minute a chance to change the world."

Dolores Huerta

To this point, we have presented information to help you develop your plan for equity. In Chapters 2 and 3, we reviewed the framework and tools of Cultural Proficiency, including the accompanying Cultural Proficiency Leadership Rubric for assessing one's readiness to lead for equity. In Chapter 4, we presented our case stories and provided the reader with practice for analyzing one case story in the context of culturally proficient practices. In this chapter, we address the development of a comprehensive plan with equity as its central focus. It is crucial to integrate plans that communicate the goals of the organization. When multiple plans exist in silos, people do not know where to direct their efforts, resources, and focus. Since this work must always be data-informed, we begin by describing some steps you can take right now to use data in an analysis of the culturally proficient practices deployed within your organization. Data provide evidence of what exists in your organization and reveal gaps that need to be acknowledged to create a plan to address the needs of your students and community. Data analysis clarifies the focus and leads to action by individuals and groups in the organization. In this way, data inform and ignite a call for change. The data are not traditional but go deeper into conditions within the organization that are preventing movement toward Cultural Proficiency. The data also identify the assets in the community that may not be known in an authentic way, to work through strengths, talents, and attributes of the people who make up the organization and its context. This book provides the foundation and inspiration to act!

YOUR NEXT STEPS: ANALYZE FOR EQUITY

Remember that Cultural Proficiency is not merely a new set of tasks, nor is it a new program to implement. Rather, it is a lens through which we see our work anew and a lens through which we can view the work that is still ahead of us. To support readers in taking the recommended actions, we have outlined eight interrelated steps. They include some traditional data points and also new data points that will instill a deeper understanding of where your organization is positioned before you move forward. It is important to determine the sequence of these steps as you prepare to develop the plan. The recommended steps are listed below and described in greater detail when addressed individually. Remember that the steps are not sequential, and it is up to you to identify what needs to be addressed first, second, and so on.

- Step one: Select data from a variety of sources.

- Step two: Disaggregate the data by significant demographic groups in your school, district, and community.

- Step three: Study longitudinal data over at least a five-year period.

- Step four: Cross-tabulate the data for demographic groups by socioeconomic status, ethnic groups, and language fluency.

- Step five: Arrange the data so they are easily read and understood by stakeholders.

- Step six: Invite stakeholders to examine the data.

- Step seven: Use data and information that stakeholders collected to explore contributing factors or hypotheses.

- Step eight: Use stakeholder input to develop an equity plan to guide your journey forward.

Each of the eight steps is explained below, with guidance for implementation. As a reminder, your organization has a unique context that will determine the order of the steps to follow and ensure that each step is considered in your plan.

STEP ONE: SELECT DATA FROM A VARIETY OF SOURCES

Data may be confusing and misleading if not looked at comprehensively. We list individual data points to assist you in beginning this crucial analysis of your organization.

First, we need to identify specific areas of information about student progress, such as those listed below. The data points listed are quantitative and will provide specific information for analysis. You may have other data points that are relevant to your school or district. Select several areas, including race, ethnicity, gender, and gender identity as components of your analysis. To go deeper, it is important to examine intersectional data points between areas. For example, in examining dropout rates, it is important to determine who is included in your dropout numbers. Are students of color dropping out? Is it students who are living in poverty or impacted by homelessness or foster care? When do you see evidence of the trend toward dropping out? It is too late to identify a student in the final years of schooling, when intervention is more difficult. Look back at reading and attendance patterns in your early grades. Research clearly identifies third grade as a benchmark. As you read the statements below, consider intersectionality of race, ethnicity, and gender under each data point.

- Achievement on standardized tests

- Dropout rates

- Earning sufficient credits to graduate on time

- Enrollment in AP or other high-status courses

- Enrollment in college-approved courses

- Enrollment in special education classes

- Enrollment trends overall

- Grade distribution

- Matriculation/graduation rates

- Parent attendance at school events

- Reclassification rates for English learners

- Suspension and expulsion data

In addition to the quantitative data you may regularly collect in your school/district, consider collecting qualitative data. Below are examples of additional qualitative data points you may collect:

- Throughout their daily schedule, shadow a high school student who is designated as an English learner or special-needs student.

- Conduct focus groups with students who are not on track to graduate, and listen to their voices.

- Meet with school counselors to learn about the concerns expressed by the students, without student identifiers.

- Observe outdoor play areas at the elementary level to see who is alone and not engaged with their peers, and keep a log of observations to see trends over time.

- At the high school level, observe the extracurricular clubs and notice which students are engaged and which students are excluded.

- When observing classrooms, note whether the environment is reflective of the student demographics.

- Collect student artifacts that illustrate student interests.

- Facilitate home visits by teachers and support personnel.

- Conduct focus groups with parents who usually do not attend school functions.

What do you know about the experience of your dropouts, including attendance, social-emotional issues, and discipline patterns? Visit your kindergarten classes on the first day of school and see if there are dramatic differences between the experiences of students as they are introduced to the start of their K–12 education. Are social-emotional supports in place across classrooms in this pivotal first learning experience?

The authors encourage you to be as comprehensive as possible. First list all the potential data sources, and next prioritize the data as you consider your short- and long-term change strategy. Paying attention to both quantitative and qualitative data will provide you with a more holistic view of the current academic and school climate of your school system to determine the next steps in creating equity goals.

STEP TWO: DISAGGREGATE THE DATA BY SIGNIFICANT DEMOGRAPHIC GROUPS IN YOUR SCHOOL, DISTRICT, AND COMMUNITY

Setting the context for examining data is a crucial part of the change process. Data are most relevant when meaningful to the stakeholders who are using the information to improve outcomes for students.

Changing mindsets around issues involving Cultural Proficiency begins at the local level. Data help confront the truth and lead to action. For example, Figure 5.1 comes from the report *Harming Our Common Future: America's Segregated Schools 65 Years After* Brown (Frankenberg et al., 2019).

FIGURE 5.1 PERCENTAGE OF INTENSELY SEGREGATED SCHOOLS, 1988–2016

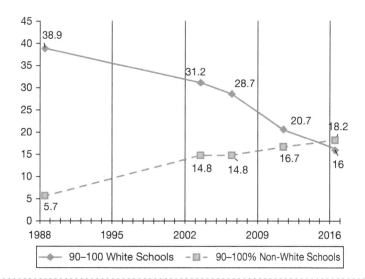

SOURCE: NCES CCD, Public Elementary/Secondary School Universe Survey Data. From The Civil Rights Project at UCLA and Center for Education and Civil Rights, *Harming Our Common Future: America's Segregated Schools 65 Years After Brown* (May 10, 2019).

As you examine Figure 5.1, what questions surface for you?

Are you experiencing increased changes in demographic patterns in your schools?

What do you know about your community?

Are you seeing any of the following patterns?

- Gentrification of communities
- Affordability of housing that is impacting where different groups live
- Homelessness of student populations
- Economic changes due to employment trends in the community
- Students new to the country due to refugee status
- Other factors

Review the listed examples in step one to make sure your examination of data is as complete as possible so it will serve to support the building of your equity plan, which will be discussed later in this chapter.

An example includes unanticipated insights from examining dropout rates. Consider data that on the surface indicate that Latinx students are underperforming in grades four through six and that the trend continues through middle and high school. When examining the data, you notice that some Latinx students are outperforming other groups. What is contributing to the success of these students? As you delve deeper into the data, you notice that students at schools that have teachers who speak Spanish are progressing consistently with a positive trajectory. You decide to examine professional development. You discuss the data with the principals of the schools and inquire if there are reasons. Principals indicate that teachers received training on scaffolding concepts for non-native speakers of English. You examine further and find that certain teachers appear to be having greater success. What is distinguishing these teachers' classrooms from those of their colleagues?

During a site visit with your district's instructional lead, you both note the similarity of practices in classrooms with teachers identified as producing greater student success. Why? The principal indicates that some of the teachers worked to implement the training and formed a community of practice. Are the teachers in the community of practice doing something different that is showing up in student outcomes?

In this example, you begin to look deeper and find important information:

- Did teachers attend training, and are there variations in implementation?

- Are teachers working together in communities of practice, and are they able to gain needed support to change their practice?

- Does classroom practice impact learning outcomes for students? Are there well-designed, research-based practices implemented with fidelity and supported by peer collaboration?

This example reinforces the importance of reflecting on local data trends and examining possible causes to help leaders establish clarity. With clarity, one begins to shape the pathway forward. The work described in this book is the "Now what?" for culturally proficient leaders. Cultural Proficiency is foundational to the plan that you will create in step eight below.

Now that you have considered the data available to you, let us move to the next step on your path to creating your equity plan and consider the importance of longitudinal data.

STEP THREE: STUDY LONGITUDINAL DATA OVER AT LEAST A FIVE-YEAR PERIOD

First, why a five-year period of study? To establish trends, research recommends five years of data to determine if patterns exist and whether they reflect changing circumstances. It can be broken down into goals and subgoals and can be distributed monthly for sixty months and reviewed annually so adjustments and updates can be made. It is important to view data over time to determine how long a trend has been in place or when it might have begun to manifest. Sometimes it may take more than five years, as the following excerpt shows.

Research by Reardon (2014) cited the growing economic inequality and the widening of the educational achievement gap between children from well-to-do families and "the children of everyone else." In fact, Reardon states that a change occurred and this gap became most evident in the period from the 1970s to the 2010s. This is critically important data because the second group of children referred to in the research describes the ones who fill most of the seats in our schools—that is, "the children of everyone else."

According to Reardon (2014), this education achievement gap "began to widen in the 1970s, right about the time that wealth and income inequality in our nation also began to grow" (p. 26). As has been said by many, *the rich get richer and the poor get poorer*, and this underscores the inequality that children and schools are facing today. It encompasses areas such as income, living arrangements, neighborhoods, and overall wealth. At the same time, the educational achievement gap became more obvious than ever before. Reardon cites that "in the 1980s, the gap between the reading and math skills of the wealthiest 10 percent of kids and poorest 10 percent was about 90 points" (p. 26). Over a thirty-year period of time, that same gap increased to 125 points.

In looking at the above citations by Reardon (2014), one can ask, "If we had paid attention to the data, would the gap have been smaller?" Other questions to assist you in your work include the following:

- Are you looking closely at your subgroups, especially where there is an intersection of students who have low achievement scores and students who live in lower socioeconomic areas?

- Have you looked at data over time for students who entered school in kindergarten and are now in fifth grade?

- Have you looked at data over time for those same students by specific subject areas?

- What do you need to do to become more knowledgeable about demographic trends?

- What else do you need to do so you are not caught off guard when you begin to see a trend developing over time?

- Using your longitudinal data, what are you doing to prepare to correct the course for your underachieving subgroups?

No one could have predicted the COVID-19 pandemic, but it is important for leaders to be agile and ready to pivot when the unexpected occurs. We see in the news comments, speculation, and data that reportedly show student achievement has suffered as a result of virtual instruction. As this is an area that has relevancy for most if not all school districts, it must be acknowledged that this is very short-term speculation that needs to be observed over time. One or two years does not tell the whole story for any group or subgroup of students, but by monitoring those data over time, we know that the impact will be long-term. Whatever the case, one cannot allow a trend to develop without studied and intentional intervention.

STEP FOUR: CROSS-TABULATE THE DATA FOR DEMOGRAPHIC GROUPS BY SOCIOECONOMIC STATUS, ETHNIC GROUPS, AND LANGUAGE FLUENCY

One example of cross-tabulation would be analyzing data about a racial or ethnic group intersected with socioeconomic data. Another example would be reviewing numbers concerning Latinx students who are English fluent intersected with *all* students who are English learners. At the same time, it is important to know that within groups you may need to disaggregate into smaller subgroups. For example, within Latinx and Asian communities, there are very distinct characteristics by socioeconomic status, culture, and language within a racial/ethnic community. In some communities, immigration status can be labeled as Latinx with the assumption that all speak Spanish, yet there are quite a few indigenous communities who may have arrived from Mexico and Central America but do not speak Spanish.

This step will assist you in determining which variables are most correlated with performance or which students most need intervention. Members of your community may want to avoid considering the correlation of racial and ethnic data with performance data. It is far more popular, and far easier, to blame everything on economic factors. Yet we know that when we cross-tabulate economic and racial/ethnic data, we find that some economically disadvantaged groups outperform their middle-class peers.

For example, it has been found that some groups of socioeconomically disadvantaged Asian students frequently outperform their white middle-class peers.

If one understands the cultural, language, and socioeconomic differences within the Asian community, one will be able to identify the unique needs for the subgroups within a specific racial/ethnic group. Two research articles address this finding. In the first, an abstract titled "Why Do Asian Americans Academically Outperform Whites? The Cultural Explanation Revisited" by Liu and Xie (2016), it was found that "Asian Americans' behaviors and attitudes are less influenced by family SES [socioeconomic status] than those of [w]hites are and that this difference helps generate Asians' premium in achievement. This is especially evident at lower levels of family SES." In an article by Michael Hotchkiss (2016), it is stated that "the research offers evidence that academic success need not be linked exclusively to a student's economic background." Liu and Xie's research is specifically cited.

It also has been found that socioeconomically disadvantaged African American and Native American students underperform compared with their Latinx and white counterparts, and in many cases African American and Native American groups are treated as though they are internally homogenous, without culturally significant distinctions of their own. In their recent review of the literature titled "Gifted Native American Students: Underperforming, Under-Identified, and Overlooked," Gentry and Fugate (2012) found that "more than 25 years later, children from low-income families and from certain cultural groups remain largely unidentified and underserved in programs for gifted and talented youth across the country. Gifted Native American children are among those most underserved in gifted education programs (Yoon & Gentry, 2009) nationally" (p. 631).

If we are going to use socioeconomic status as a variable, we need to know which socioeconomically disadvantaged students are most at risk. A significant amount of data show that, when it comes to school performance, race and ethnicity are often more important than economic class. Cross-tabulation controls for such conditions and gives us more precise information about where to target our interventions.

STEP FIVE: ARRANGE THE DATA SO THEY ARE EASILY READ AND UNDERSTOOD BY STAKEHOLDERS

Accurate and easy-to-read reports are as important as the data they contain. Be sure to format your information in a way that makes your findings clear and impactful. Bar graphs work well when comparing progress among groups, as do pie charts. It is best to avoid raw numbers or scores that must be calculated to determine a trend. Presentation of data can start at the aggregate level by subgroups. It should include data that are disaggregated at the level representative of the student's current status, but not their full potential.

Figure 5.2 is an example of state data at an aggregate level by racial/ethnic subgroups. A quick glance would indicate that all Asians, Filipinos, those of two or more races, and whites score above average on state assessments. What it does not show, for all groups, is the data that are missing across other data points: gender, subgroups within racial/ethnic groups listed, socioeconomic status, single-family households, foster youth, special education, homelessness, and more.

FIGURE 5.2 CALIFORNIA STUDENTS WHO MET STATE STANDARDS IN 2019

	ENGLISH	MATH
Asian	76.86%	74.37%
Filipino	71.37%	59.52%
Two or more races	65.52%	55.26%
White	65.42%	54.23%
Hawaiian/Pacific Islander	43.39%	32.60%
Latino	40.56%	28.05%
Native American	38.16%	26.58%
Black	33.02%	20.55%

SOURCE: Data from California Department of Education.

It is important to acknowledge the uniqueness of each racial/ethnic group to provide the appropriate support for the educational attainment.

To illustrate the concern of categorizing one demographic of the Asian American and Pacific Islander (AAPI) population, Figure 5.3 shows the diversity of the entire AAPI community. Yet, as noted in the California State Department of Education data in Figure 5.2, "Asian" was listed as one homogeneous group.

As a state, if we look only at the Asian aggregate assessment data, California can be proud of the academic achievement of Asian students, but if disaggregated by high school completion and Southeast Asian American subgroups, the data would not be impressive. Figure 5.4 disaggregates the data more closely by specific racial/ethnic groups and by high school attainment.

The next level of data analysis would include the socioeconomic status of the racial/ethnic groups listed in the figure. At the same time, it is important to know that within groups you may need to disaggregate into smaller subgroups.

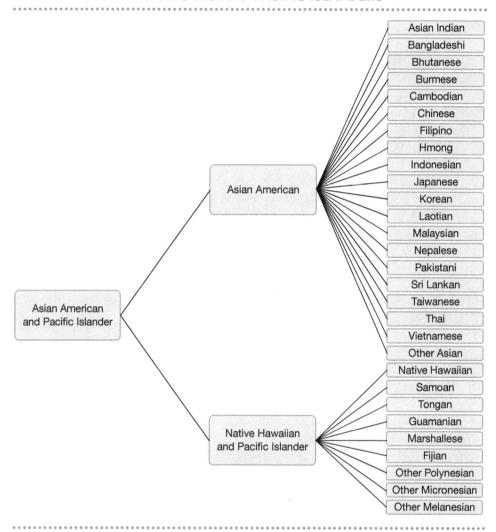

SOURCE: U.S. Census Bureau, 2010. Copyright © 2013 ETS. www.ets.org. Figures from iCount: A Data Quality Movement for Asian American are reprinted by permission of ETS, the copyright owner. All other information contained within this publication is provided by Corwin Press, Inc. and no endorsement of any kind by ETS should be inferred.

Figure 5.4 is an example of data that lead to deeper understanding of what you know about your students by including other variables and analyzing the data trends. Acknowledging the educational attainment of the Hmong, Cambodian, Laotian, and Vietnamese, there needs to be an expectation that an equity goal for these students would be different than for Taiwanese, Japanese, and continuing on with other groups. This micro data analysis must be done for all groups. If relying on only the aggregate for subgroups we regularly include in a report, we miss the opportunity to know, respect, and support all students in our system. As we share these data, it helps our stakeholders understand the importance of doing this work with a Cultural

FIGURE 5.4 EDUCATIONAL ATTAINMENT FOR ASIAN AMERICAN SUBGROUPS, 2008–2010

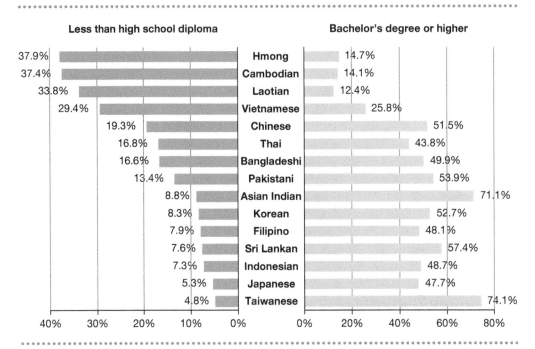

SOURCE: U.S. Census Bureau, American Community Survey. Copyright © 2013 ETS. www.ets.org. Figures from iCount: A Data Quality Movement for Asian American are reprinted by permission of ETS, the copyright owner. All other information contained within this publication is provided by Corwin Press, Inc. and no endorsement of any kind by ETS should be inferred.

Proficiency lens to meet the educational and social-emotional needs of the rich diversity of our community.

STEP SIX: INVITE STAKEHOLDERS TO EXAMINE THE DATA

It is important to expose members of your staff to these data. It will open their eyes to the trends that are present but hidden within their schools, and it will give them an opportunity to contribute to a more equitable school system from the very start. Ask them:

• What trends do you notice?

• Are the trends visible over a specific period of time?

• What trends do you notice for which demographic groups?

• Are some groups improving?

• Are gaps closing?

Which questions do they feel are most essential, and why? The following suggestions will help you navigate your stakeholder discussions.

Working With the Stakeholders

- At first, do not let stakeholders posit why they think the data are the way they are.

- Instead, ask stakeholders, "What do you observe in the data? What story do the data seem to be telling?"

- Ask the stakeholders what they know about the student groups associated with the data. What are they surprised to see in the data? Capture their words to help shape the story you are crafting for your equity plan (see step eight).

- When thinking about the root causes of the data you find, ask yourself whether there are other variables the stakeholders may need to know about in advance. Keep removing the layers until you identify the variables and the root causes. Once you have credible data, you can move forward with confidence and speed.

- After reviewing the data, ask the stakeholders what they believe is needed to know about specific student groups, curriculum content, methods of instruction, assessment, teacher competence, and school rules. Be sure to emphasize consistency when it comes to educator practice. Consider ways you measure consistency. Ask questions about what is happening in your school or district. For example, does your school or district use data walks as part of its regular practice? Is there a safe culture for trying new classroom strategies that come from research-based professional development strategies for the classroom that target student learning issues?

- Provide a set period of time, preferably time that is already part of the calendar, for instructional conversations. In this new era of virtual meetings, make this accommodation available to include parents and other key stakeholders. This effort demonstrates that the work is core to improvement and is a priority for everyone. Together, you and your stakeholders can investigate variables that might shed light on the performance data.

- Consider working with a small planning team of key leaders to shape how the data will be introduced. If your team is familiar with using data to examine student progress, they will see the connection to disaggregating information in new ways. They may even suggest additional approaches to get the most meaning out of the session. Approach this initial data session as building on what the team already does, but now using new tools to promote greater success for all students.

- Consider the following sequence for your meetings. Note that your context may require more than one session for each.

  1. First meeting to introduce the existing data

  2. Second meeting to delve deeper into the data and begin to ask questions about the data presented at the first meeting

  3. Third meeting to provide critical time and space for participants to explore possible factors impacting outcomes

  4. Fourth meeting to establish action steps

Anticipate excuses, as change is difficult and defensiveness is a common response. Staff may want to blame the students, parents, lack of resources, and poverty in the community. Do not be put off by excuses that represent cultural incompetency. You are on a journey to improve outcomes for all students, and that means changing the biases that adults bring to the classroom and school. Helping your team see the potential in students may mean opening their minds to unlearn excuses and embrace the opportunity to demonstrate their ability to impact learning and achievement.

As a practice, consider having a parallel conversation with schools examining their specific data. Ensure your principals are prepared to lead discussions about student performance, to ask questions that will lead to meaningful conversations, and to guide accurate interpretation of data.

For example, at an urban high school, faculty are examining the difference in performance between biology classes. This high school serves a demographic mix of African American and Latinx students. Teachers newer to the profession who were recruited from local universities share examples of their students' work to get feedback on how they can improve their instruction. Teachers who have been at the school for ten or more years share work examples that are significantly below standard. During the conversation, experienced teachers say that students cannot meet the objective. Beginning teachers state that they feel their students are doing well, but they still want to get even higher performance. What is going on in this conversation? How can leaders provide opportunities for teachers to examine work in safe and authentic ways to encourage improvement of practice and outcomes? How often do these conversations happen in your school, district, or organization?

Another example finds a school system that serves a large population of English learners struggling to adjust to using remote or hybrid learning. Teachers are uncertain about the best ways to develop English skills while working to get students to use their computers to log on for class time. Many teachers indicate that students are falling behind in their English language development, resulting in lasting negative impact on their long-term achievement. The superintendent identifies an expert from a local university who helps teachers understand that the bilingual strategies that support communication and content also predispose the English learner to the cognitive flexibility needed for both synchronous and asynchronous learning. The teachers work with the expert to identify software for language tutoring and practice strategies to maximize learning in the virtual classroom. As teachers focus on how they will track student growth, they are doing the "Now what?" work of using data to open their minds to new ways of teaching and learning. Their fear of teaching in the online classroom grows into productive problem-solving about their students and their teaching practice.

As you invite stakeholders to examine data, you are helping them use the most powerful tool to change education and society. Data reveal the truth, and using data can change schools and society.

STEP SEVEN: USE DATA AND INFORMATION THAT STAKEHOLDERS COLLECTED TO EXPLORE CONTRIBUTING FACTORS OR HYPOTHESES

As you share data with your stakeholders, many will want to discuss the "why" of the outcomes and find a reason, cause, and/or excuse for the data they see. Schools tend to look outward to the causes and do not spend time looking at the variables schools can control.

The three variables we control relate to the knowledge we have, the attitudes and motivation we bring to the school setting, and systemic or organizational barriers we encounter in the schools (Rueda, 2011).

We begin with being honest regarding the knowledge we have about students, and not just our assumptions. Do we care enough to take the time to truly know the students we teach, lead, and support?

- Knowledge that teachers and others have or do not have about students, their preparedness, learning or cultural styles or needs, quality of resources, articulated curriculum, home factors such as food insecurity, parents' presence in the home, living conditions, and health issues. It is important for each of us to determine what is known and what needs to be known about our students and community. Specific areas of knowing include these:

- Assumptions that school staff make based on visible conditions, such as assuming a student is from one racial/ethnic group or assuming the pronouns of a student who identifies as LGBTQ+ but has not shared their gender identity. These assumptions can be inaccurate and may be harmful to students. Every student has a story. Efforts need to be made to know the child and determine if any invisible factors are influencing their performance. Students need to know you care and are there to support their success.

- Knowledge of appropriate pedagogy for students and willingness to learn about a student's cultural background to enhance curricular choices. Not all knowledge is Eurocentric.

- The ability to reflect on one's own knowledge to adapt to meet the needs of diverse communities.

- Looking inward and becoming aware of one's own bias toward specific racial groups, socioeconomic status, or gender identity.

- Accessing the knowledge that resides within the community to support your equity work.

• Motivation is critical to the success of school personnel and their desire to support diverse learners. Motivation includes self-efficacy and confidence in doing the work, and willingness to take risks with clear goals and expectations. Below are examples of motivational influences:

- Take responsibility for educating the whole child based on where they are, and ensure that their unique needs are acknowledged and addressed.

- Be willing to be a learner with your students to increase confidence and provide the appropriate interventions.

- Employ strategies such as community mapping to help teachers understand the assets that the child and the community bring to the classroom.

The organizational culture (shift) creates the conditions for meaningful exchange between groups within the district. Mutual respect is foundational to building an organizational culture to support equity work.

- Systemic or organizational barriers are the values and beliefs that are infused throughout the organization, such as trust, support for innovation, and allowing people to take risks. They also include policies and regulations that inhibit and/or support students and teachers to be their best. Listed below are reflective questions to consider:
  - Is there a cultural model of no excuses and high expectations for both teachers and students in the system?
  - Are there specific discipline policies that are harmful to students?
  - How are values communicated to teachers, students, and the community?
  - Does organizational culture support teacher capacity to learn?
  - Does the organization provide the necessary resources and time to remove the barriers and help teachers feel competent and ready to succeed?
  - Does the system provide opportunities for people to come together in small groups to discuss progress in reaching the aspirations described in your shared vision and beliefs?
  - Do avenues exist in the work setting for individuals to share their frustrations without judgment? Do they feel heard?

Understanding the three variables that impact student performance will help you begin to develop your equity plan with specific goals and metrics. The "Now what?" of the work begins!

STEP EIGHT: USE STAKEHOLDER INPUT TO DEVELOP AN EQUITY PLAN TO GUIDE YOUR JOURNEY FORWARD

Importance of the Equity Plan

The equity plan (going forward, referred to as *the plan*) to guide your journey is crucial to your success. Without a plan, how do you or your stakeholders know where you are heading? The authors recommend communicating your vision and mission for your organization to keep your team focused as the plan is developed. The plan needs to involve broad stakeholder representation so you maximize commitment across your school or organization. This plan should reflect what you learned in examining your local data and exploring other factors that influence outcomes for students.

Do not delay creating the plan after you complete the data analysis process, as this will send a message that you and the organization are not serious about the urgency of this work. It is a natural transition to move from examining data to taking the "Now what?" step.

Stakeholders may be cautious because a plan equates to change, and change can be intimidating, especially during divisive politics and social unrest. On the other hand, the plan can be the greatest positive factor in ensuring your success, as it identifies the work and, through the work, the change that is needed. Research confirms that goal clarity is a key element in organizational success. The plan brings stakeholders together with shared purpose and clarity of direction.

Telling Your Story

The authors provide the example from the documentary *Let the Little Light Shine*, by Kevin Shaw (2022), which captures the story of a K–8 school with an equity agenda serving a predominately Black population in South Chicago. This public school, located near the former Harold Ickes public housing project, had a staff that was beloved by the community and could best be characterized as believing in their students and motivating them to excel and distinguish themselves and their school. As gentrification comes to their community, the school is threatened with closure. The work of all stakeholders to prevent the closure is inspirational and serves as a reminder of the power of equity work and how it can transform a school and community. The documentary is included only as an example and reminder that equity work is powerful and transformative. You will have your own examples, and the authors encourage you to continue to keep a record of your story and the Cultural Proficiency journey you are taking with your internal and external stakeholders. Your equity work will bring people together with a shared sense of purpose that reflects the knowledge, motivation, and organizational factors that are discussed in step seven above. Your plan will capture the ingredients that show the way forward and serve as your shining light for the future.

The Equity Plan

The equity plan is not a separate plan that lives in its own space. It needs to be woven into the strategic plan that provides direction for your school, district, or organization. Capture the challenging work described in steps one through seven, including delving deeply into the data, exploring root causes, and forming hypotheses for the outcomes you are seeking. Involving both internal and external stakeholders who can help support the work and share accurate communication about the plan and steps you will develop below is critical to the process. Consider a specific stakeholder, such as parents.

For example, not every parent has the time to attend meetings, so consider how to communicate your journey with periodic reports to the community. Use the new virtual platforms that have shown increased participation at public meetings as a way to bring more people together for the discussion and planning process. Make sure to reach out to external stakeholders, such as elected officials, service clubs, churches, other nonprofit organizations, realtors, and wrap-around service providers, all of whom have an interest in the success of your efforts. As you develop your plan, consider your context, as this will help you determine specific approaches.

Your plan should communicate your vision and mission for your school, district, or organization and should reflect the voices of your internal and external stakeholders. The authors encourage you to review the template below and make modifications that reflect your context.

Equity Plan Ingredients

- State your vision and mission for children in your school, district, or organization and describe who was involved.

  o _____

  o _____

- Describe your data analysis process.

  o _____

  o _____

- List root causes you identified in step seven.

  o _____

  o _____

- List the top two to three priority areas you plan to tackle first.

  o _____

  o _____

(Continued)

(Continued)

- For each area, identify the initial steps you plan to implement.

  o _____

  o _____

- Establish timelines, and identify those accountable for each step.

  o _____

  o _____

- List key communication strategies to share the process with your internal and external stakeholders (who does what).

  o _____

  o _____

- List the potential challenges that could undermine your plan, and begin to anticipate possible solutions.

  o _____

  o _____

- Celebrate your successes.

  o _____

  o _____

As your plan comes together, take time to reflect with your team and celebrate the first steps to advancing your equity agenda and commitment to excellence for *all*. This plan communicates your moral imperative and binds you and your team together to address and overcome challenges and celebrate your successes!

CONCLUSION: IT IS WHAT YOU *DO* THAT MATTERS

The above steps should assist you in your work of developing a plan, but we want to remind you of the personal and human dimensions of this work. While planning is essential for realizing effective action, schools frequently engage in planning that leads nowhere. It is what you *do*, not what you write or say, that will have the greatest constructive impact on your professional practice and, thereby, on your students and their communities.

The good news is that there are many action steps you can take immediately, including creating readiness for this work in yourself and in others. Since the work requires an *inside-out approach,* we the authors want to stress the importance of preparing yourself and others by developing a strengths-based mindset. This preparation is necessary for challenging the deficit thinking that so often plagues our school systems. Readiness can be fostered through interpersonal and intergroup dialogue, common readings, and discussions of appropriate resources, or through other training. Continuing support for stakeholders as they progress through the eight steps will ensure that all are ready to engage in this equity work. It is essential that you focus on the human dimension by

- always leading from the heart,

- being compassionate and empathetic,

- modeling a growth mindset,

- beginning where people are and nurturing forward movement from that point, and

- aspiring to be a culturally proficient leader—*it is a lifelong journey!*

There are many intersections in our lives, but the most important one is the place where our heart and passion intersect with our will and action—this is where we do our best work.

CHAPTER 6

....

LEADERSHIP FOR TRANSFORMATION . . . THE TIME IS NOW

"Ours is not the struggle of one day, one week, or one year. Ours is not the struggle of one judicial appointment or presidential term. Ours is the struggle of a lifetime, or maybe even many lifetimes, and each one of us in every generation must do our part."

John Lewis

Change in education requires that we modify our day-to-day actions. Transformation, however, requires that we modify our core beliefs and long-term behaviors in profound ways. At its core, this is what Cultural Proficiency is about—transforming your work and education in profound ways to achieve results that seemed otherwise elusive or impossible. This chapter is designed for you to reflect on three questions that will help you and those you work with transform education for equitable results:

1. What *knowledge* do you have or need to have?

2. What *skills* do you have or need to cultivate?

3. How strong is your *will* to stay the course?

However, before examining these questions, we must clarify the driving force behind this work—the *why* of striving for equitable education. Make no mistake: only one thing can truly compel it. Michael Fullan in 2003 described it as a *moral imperative* or *purpose*, which is still relevant today:

> You don't have to go very far into the question of the role of public schools in a democracy before discovering that moral purpose is at the heart of the matter. As the main institution for fostering social cohesion in an increasingly diverse society, publicly funded schools must serve all children, not simply those with the loudest or most powerful advocates. This means addressing the cognitive and social needs of all children, with an emphasis on including those who may not have been well-served in the past. (p. 3)

For too many years, schools have focused on kids who come to school already equipped with the resources and opportunities necessary to be successful, while at the same time failing the students who most need their help. We should be outraged, but not without purpose. Our outrage fuels our desire to serve all the children in our schools, whatever their needs. It puts us in touch with why we do this work. Purposefully embracing that outrage and transforming it into positive change for our students constitutes our starting point for this work. The moral imperative of bettering the lives of our students constitutes our *why*. But such work does not happen in a vacuum. The *why* of equitable education is naturally embedded in the environment that makes it necessary. Recent events, as well as long-standing political realities in our communities, are where our purpose takes root. This is the context in which we begin.

THE CONTEXT: INFLECTION POINTS AND THE NEED FOR ACTIVISM

An inflection point is a critical time that results in a significant change in the character of a society, an industry, or an organization. It can be intentional or an accidental harbinger of positive or negative change and can, therefore, be seen as either advantageous (for organizations willing and able to change) or disastrous (for organizations without the will or skill to adapt). In recent years our nation has witnessed several inflection points in the form of unprecedented turmoil centered on race and gender. Black Lives Matter demonstrations, #MeToo protests, and other social movements focused on raising awareness about social justice and human rights issues have sown seeds of social upheaval and political resistance.

Recent polls indicate that Black Lives Matter may be the largest social movement in U.S. history. Since its inception in 2013, the movement has surged, and while it concentrates on criminal justice reform for African Americans, it also represents many views and amplifies an array of voices, among them LGBTQ+ activists and advocates for immigration reform. The fuel behind the movement also has been multicultural and multiracial. Not only are

African Americans and other marginalized people fighting for justice, but large segments of non-marginalized advocates are simultaneously calling for an examination and rebalancing of the power structures embedded in society and its institutions.

In this way, Black Lives Matter is part of an evolving philosophy known as anti-racism, which has roots in America as far back as the seventeenth century. In its present form, anti-racism takes an explicitly activist stance against historical systemic oppression of any kind. Black Lives Matter and anti-racism are concerned with more than *not being racist*: as philosophies, they stress the necessity of being *anti-racist* and actively confronting oppression wherever it is found. As Ibram X. Kendi (2019) explains, anti-racism is not just about ending racism and other forms of oppression; it is also about restructuring society and rebalancing power.

It is important to understand that oppression takes many forms, and our nation has much to account for in its past and present. While some forms are more historically and perniciously embedded in our society, oppression is always oppression, regardless of the targeted group, and all forms of oppression require the same dedication to activism found among advocacy groups like Black Lives Matter.

From among the voices demanding justice comes a clarion call for hope and collective action for realizing the egalitarian vision of inclusivity, democracy, and justice. At the same time, there are groups who are threatened by shifting power structures and racial equity. They are pushing back with counter-campaigns, counter-protests, and counter-legislation aimed at debilitating schools that teach the history of race truthfully or that prioritize equitable pedagogy of any kind, whether it be about the history of racism in the United States or the importance of social–emotional learning.

So what do we *do*? What role should schools play in our society? Do we see the recent inflection points around race and social justice as opportunities for change, or are we intimidated by the counter-campaigns that seek to silence marginalized voices and their advocates? Howard (2020), faculty director for UCLA's Center for the Transformation of Schools, urges schools to remain steadfast and to translate the energy of the ongoing protests into concrete actions:

> If schools are really serious about addressing anti-Black racism beyond this mainstream moment then there will have to be a much greater investment in different policies, practices, and beliefs when the fervor dissipates. When the marches stop, schools will need to look at themselves hard in the mirror and ask, how can we say Black Lives Matter when we are complicit in Black student failure? When the protests come to an end, schools will have to ask

themselves, how can we state that we want to end systemic racism when many policies disproportionately punish, suspend and systematically fail Black students? . . . In short, this moment makes it easy for schools to say that Black Lives Matter. This moment has made it comfortable for schools to say that racism is real and that they will stand up against it, but when the lights go down, will schools do the really heavy lifting to examine school curriculum which often excludes Black history, life and culture?

The Education Trust-West reports that "race matters. And racial equity should be at the center of every single decision being made about what students need to thrive. Yet 25 years ago California's universities stopped using race as a factor in determining student admissions after the ban on affirmative action" (Nellum, 2021, p. 1). As a result,

- Latinx students make up more than half of the state's public high school seniors and just under half of all California State University (CSU) undergraduates;
- only around half of Black public high school graduates go on to a non-state college;
- only three in ten Native American students who graduate public high school in California are eligible to apply to a University of California or CSU school, and as a result, only about 13 percent of Native adults in California hold bachelor's degrees; and
- while about 51 percent of all Asian Americans over the age of twenty-five have a bachelor's degree or greater, outcomes vary greatly by ethnic group. For example, in the Cambodian and Hmong communities, only 18 percent and 17 percent, respectively, have a bachelor's degree (Nellum, 2021, p. 1).

Evidence such as this makes it clear, and history further clarifies: transforming schools for equity is an urgent task. Gaps in education, if unchecked, turn into a variety of social ills and gaps that disproportionately affect people of color and minorities, including gaps in earnings, health care, insurance, employability, wellness, and housing. Closing these gaps and tending to these ills is today's work, but it will not be easy. It will be perhaps the hardest work you will undertake in your lifetime. It is not for the faint of heart or for those who are easily offended. To succeed, you will need to anticipate resistance and denial and perhaps even face sabotage. Expect to be uncomfortable and to make others uncomfortable. But know that this work, this long educational struggle that persists, is a fight that is worth everyone's time and effort. It is literally for the greater good.

We now return to the questions mentioned at the beginning of the chapter. The first step toward equitable education for your students is self-examination. What do you need to know? What skills do you have, and what skills will you need? And what can you do to sustain your will to do this work?

KNOWLEDGE: WHAT DO YOU ALREADY KNOW, AND WHAT DO YOU NEED TO KNOW?

One thing we can do as anti-racist educators is demand disaggregated data about racial groups in our schools. Do they receive equal access to and opportunities for challenging, culturally relevant coursework? Are certain groups disciplined disproportionately? Do all your students have access to the same basic services? Do they all have the same after-school opportunities, and if not, why?

Below are two examples from the COVID-19 pandemic that are still relevant beyond the crisis and address the knowledge school staff should have or should learn about their students and community. These two examples cut across the Cultural Proficiency Leadership Rubric, from assessing cultural knowledge to institutionalizing cultural knowledge.

Schools focused on providing effective intervention to address the learning loss of many students. An analysis of the Understanding America Study in 2020–2021 by Saavedra and Polikoff (2021) found that the interventions offered to parents were not well received. The offerings ranged from summer school to tutoring after school. The study found only 3 to 10 percent of parents were enrolling in the programs offered by the districts. The authors also found that parents felt online learning was useful and should continue. The key finding was that school personnel should first engage parents to learn what would be helpful to their children. The authors concluded, "What these results make clear is that education leaders need to talk to parents to figure out what programs and policies they would support and participate in before simply creating COVID-19-relief programs using rescue plan dollars. Otherwise, participation may be far too weak to really move the needle on students' academic and social/emotional needs." Thus, it is important schools engage parents in authentic discussion about what they believe their children need. Oftentimes, schools assume that parents will support the activities offered by the school, without addressing the needs of both parents and students. Schools must take the time to get to know their students and students' families if the goal is to meet the academic and social–emotional needs of all students.

A nonprofit organization working with Oakland Unified School District found that reimagining the role of a community/family liaison can be a model going forward for all schools that want to use the knowledge of their community to engage parents and students in meaningful and productive ways (Daramola, 2021). In a policy report by the USC Rossier School of Education, Center on Educational Policy, Equity and Governance, *Centering the Family in the Family Liaison Role,* Daramola (2021) highlights key findings that empowered parents to become activists for their children. The report provides an in-depth study of Oakland Reach, which created a virtual hub to help Black and Latinx families navigate COVID-19 learning. The author concludes that schools must reframe the family liaison role to focus on supporting and empowering parents, not on school goals such as improving attendance. The findings indicate that when parents are in the driver's seat, schools might see an increase in student outcomes such as attendance and academic achievement. Family liaisons should support the needs of families to ensure parents are knowledgeable about the school system and the important role parents play in their child's life. The author states, "Leaders should consider how schools might improve if educators are required to attend to the advocacy of Black and Latinx parents at the same rate as [w]hite and affluent parents" (p. 9). Schools should lead with an asset mindset for their community, and family liaisons can help schools develop this equity lens for all school personnel (Daramola, 2021).

We must be careful not to settle for data about improvement or be swayed by positive but superficial narratives about success. While parents, principals, and the public all love improvement data, these data often hide an ugly truth about persisting educational gaps between white and historically marginalized students. Closing and eliminating such gaps is the only way to ensure we are making progress toward an egalitarian, emancipatory society, especially in our schools.

Since 1971, in what is often referred to as the Nation's Report Card, the National Assessment of Educational Progress has documented, measured, and reported on achievement gaps between white and marginalized students every two years (Perie et al., 2005). School reform efforts have poured from the offices of government officials at the state and federal level for more than four decades. No Child Left Behind and, in California, for example, the Local Control Accountability Plan required schools receiving Title I funds to be accountable for better educating children they identified as underserved. However, in many schools, including our best colleges and universities, it is as if achievement gaps were only recently discovered. Or these gaps are treated as irrelevant to the day-to-day work of classroom teachers, many of whom want to make their own instructional decisions based on their past school experiences. So even when data concerning achievement and opportunity gaps are available, fear of the unknown, fear of too much additional work, ignorance about what works best, and lack of personal conviction can get in the way of forward movement.

To push through these manifestations of resistance, you must strive to know more about yourself and your school, from the classroom level to the central office. You can begin by taking an inventory and asking yourself these fundamental questions:

- What do you know about your organization's status quo? Do teachers tend to follow recommendations gathered from analysis? Or do they tend to resist recommended changes?

- What do you know about your organization's ability to meet the needs of *all* its students?

- What data do you collect and review? What data have you failed to collect that you need?

- Have your demographics shifted, resulting in a change in student performance? For example, is gentrification taking place in a neighborhood in the district or at a particular school? Has there been a change in ethnic or racial demographics at particular grade levels?

- Where do you see gaps appearing? For which students? Typical gaps include these: African American male students are the lowest performing students of all groups, and a subgroup of Asian American students outperforms white students. For how long? Examination should include whether this is a recent change or one that occurred over time. Has there been improvement over time? Are gaps closing and for which students? For which groups?

- What trends stand out for you as they relate to historically underserved students?

- To what extent do stakeholders know about these trends, and more important, to what extent do they care enough to do what is necessary to narrow and close educational gaps? Have they failed to address them in the past?

- Are you aware of any deficit beliefs among your staff that are barriers to teaching and learning?

- Do you know who your students are, and do you understand their needs? Does your school or district attend to their cultural and linguistic learning needs?

- What do you know about the cultures within your community? How can you leverage that to improve communication and trust?

- Do you know about the common cultural clashes between the communities in your school?

- How much do you know about the Culturally Proficient Framework? Do you know which tools in the framework you can use to leverage change?

SKILL: WHAT CAN YOU DO, AND WHAT MUST YOU LEARN TO DO?

Data can tell us a great deal about the effectiveness of our organizations. They give us a starting point and, especially among decision-makers, provide an impetus to *do whatever it takes* to close gaps. Data tell us how hard or easy the job will be, and data help prioritize efforts so we can work with the children who need our attention most. The culturally proficient leader must be passionate about or develop a passion for data. They must possess and develop in others high data literacy and data capacity. Stakeholders must learn and use the language of data.

Effective leaders know how to retrieve data from multiple sources, interpret it, and rearrange it so it is understandable to stakeholders. Effective equity leaders disaggregate data, cross-tabulate it to further identify students most in need of intervention, and implement longitudinal studies to determine the historical trends and trajectories of student success. Leaders and staff must be comfortable working with data to hold themselves and others accountable for progress. Data should not be perceived as negative. They can provide neutral information to help inform programs, decisions, and resource allocations, and they must be an ongoing part of the managerial repertoire alongside the moral impetus we described earlier. Data are a necessary tool but can be a misleading one as well, and the effective equity leader must know where the most common pitfalls lie.

Can you facilitate group dynamics and mediate conflict? Culturally proficient leaders know the difference between skillful discussion and dialogue and when to use each effectively. Leaders build and maintain safe environments for people to discuss difficult, often controversial, topics, and they know how to challenge ideas without humiliating participants. They know how to reframe deficit beliefs and empower staff to work with the strengths their students bring to their classrooms. Culturally proficient leaders have an agenda for equity but know how to remain emotionally neutral in the midst of cultural conflict. Leaders build networks, coalitions, and bridges between and among constituent groups. They know how to build cohesion and how to resolve cultural clashes. Leaders can, and often *do*, admit their mistakes.

Intergroup Dialogue

Over the past ten years there has been much research on the topics of "courageous conversations" and "managing conflict." The authors would like to introduce you to a process known as intergroup dialogue (Yeakley & Brett, 2020; Zúñiga et al., 2002, 2007). The first intergroup dialogue program began in 1988 at the University of Michigan, in response to racist incidents and student protests. The process of intergroup dialogue is an evidence model and has expanded to many universities, high schools, and communities across the country (Yeakely & Brett, 2020). This approach establishes a four-stage model of intergroup dialogue as cited in the research above and as listed below.

- **Stage one: Setting the ground for engagement.** Building the capacity for engagement and getting acquainted.

- **Stage two: Exploring identities and inequalities.** Exploring commonalities and differences in socialization, contextualizing identities and relationships in systems of inequalities.

- **Stage three: Engaging in controversial issues.** Exploring dimensions of personal and political issues, engaging in disagreements and differences on political issues.

- **Stage four: Alliance building and action planning.** Strengthening collaborative relationships, engaging individually and collectively in social action and change.

The first lesson is to understand the differences among dialogue, discussion, and debate. Table 6.1 was adapted by Yeakley and Brett (2020).

The key to successful intergroup dialogue is active listening. We must be present and be thoughtful in our responses. We also must be aware of our positionality and the power dynamics in the relationship to have participants fully engaged. In addition, it is important to provide opportunities to explore our commonalities and systems of equality, and to exhibit a willingness to engage in courageous/difficult conversation and come together for social action and change (Yeakley & Brett, 2020; Zúñiga et al., 2002, 2007).

WILL: DO YOU HAVE THE WILL TO TAKE THE JOURNEY TO CULTURAL PROFICIENCY?

Advocating for social justice and educational equity requires a strong moral center and a dedication to scrutinizing both your own convictions and what you learn about your school as you strive to help your most vulnerable students. Therefore, advocating for social justice is not about what others do or

TABLE 6.1 WHAT IS DIALOGUE?

WHAT IS DIALOGUE? (VERSUS DEBATE, DISCUSSION)		
DIALOGUE	**DEBATE**	**DISCUSSION**
Broaden own perspective	Succeed or win	Present ideas
Look for shared meaning	Look for weakness	Seek answers or solutions
Find places of agreement	Stress disagreement	Persuade others
Allow for and invite differences of opinion and experience	Advocate one perspective or another	Solve our own and others' problems
Challenge our and others' preconceived notions	Judge other viewpoints as inferior or invalid	Achieve preset goals

SOURCE: Adapted by Anna Yeakley and Teresa Brett, from *Comparison of Dialogue and Debate* (Berman, 1993), *Differentiating Dialogue From Discussion: A Working Model* (Kardin & Sevig, 1997), and *Exploring the Differences Between Dialogue, Discussion, and Debate* (Kachwaha, 2002, adapted from Huang-Nissan, 1999)

do not do. It is about our own determination to advocate for and meet the needs of historically underserved students. We mentioned earlier that a *moral imperative* drives our work and helps us stay on course. We can check our adherence to the moral imperative, to the centrality of our students' needs, by reflecting one of the guiding principles for Cultural Proficiency: *People are served in varying degrees by the dominant culture.* Leaders who believe in this principle and who can facilitate an understanding about it across all stakeholder groups will have a much easier time laying the foundation for the moral imperative and will have an easier time generating the commitment and resolution necessary to do this work.

Leaders who have *will* do not allow themselves to get stuck in the *whats* and *hows*. They use the data-gathering period to build buy-in and ensure success. This process was reviewed in Chapter 5. The timeline for completing the eight steps outlined is typically a six-to-twelve-month process. A leader will launch the work with a diverse group of key stakeholders. This will be the board and senior staff in the traditional school district but could include others in a charter network or educational organization. You are working toward the goal of establishing your plan and action steps, so do not rush the process due to your sense of urgency. Begin speaking about the long-term goals while establishing a solid foundation to anchor your work. You will realize that the work you communicate, although in the early stages, will lead to improved outcomes for students. Remember that what the leader emphasizes and communicates gets attention.

Leaders for equity know how to seed support from various constituency groups, and they consistently analyze outcomes and impact as they move forward. The leader is building the team with a critical mass of individuals who share the vision for equity work and understand the impact of a culturally proficient system. They know which barriers may need to be removed along the way and how to remove them. Leaders inspire others with their own *will* and passion, and cultivate excitement and commitment in others. Equity leaders draw out the best in others because they understand that human effort and success come from clarity of purpose and goals. They build the team because they understand that progress is achieved with shared commitment and relentless pursuit of answers to the challenges they face. They know the research about diverse teams and the positive impact that comes when all voices have a place at the table, where respect for diverse points of view is modeled. Equity leaders communicate a personal and collective commitment *to do whatever it takes,* and they create the conditions for trust and success.

This sense of *will* can be seen in the actions of Rabbi Heschel. Returning from the Selma march in 1965, he was asked if he found much time to pray. He responded, "I prayed with my feet." The image of taking action by continuing to walk reinforces the importance of moving forward while establishing the foundation for success. *Will* can be seen in the life of John Lewis. Despite the incredible violence that he and other protesters encountered on the Edmund Pettus Bridge, despite a skull fracture inflicted on him by white police officers, *he kept his eyes on the prize*: the passage of the Civil Rights Act. Social justice work requires courage, especially during a period of social unrest. The physical pain endured by John Lewis is symbolic of the emotional toll you may encounter as you do this important work. *Will* is Jaime Escalante's relentless pursuit to obtain quality texts for his students in defiance of his administration, who refused his requests by responding, "No, Jaime, those books do not qualify for Title I. They are clearly not remedial" and "Jaime, if you get better test scores for these kids then we're not going to qualify for Title I money" (Escalante, 1990, p. 410).

In his provocatively titled article "Do We Have the Will to Educate All Children?" Asa Hilliard III (1991, p. 34) focuses on the moral dimension of education by emphasizing the potential that children *and educators* embody. He writes that "a *deep restructuring* is a matter of drawing up an appropriate vision of human potential, of aiming for the stars for the children and for ourselves academically and socially. . . . Just as there is a vast untapped potential, yes, genius among the children, there is also a vast untapped potential among the teachers who serve those children" (p. 35). The *will* to do equity work is present in that untapped potential, in the genius of the entire community. Leaders work toward freeing that genius as they deepen their knowledge, nurture their skills, and spread their passion for equitable education among their staff. *Will*, in this sense, is not just steadfastness, passion, or tireless work. It is also the desire to see the promise of public education fulfilled in and through others. The authors shared tools in previous chapters to support you as you undertake the equity journey, but most important, the authors connect with your passion, commitment, and unrelenting determination to make a positive and lasting change for children who have not been served well by the system in the past.

CLOSING THOUGHTS

We invite our readers to join us in taking personal responsibility for realizing the democratic core of public education so all children and youth receive the education they need and deserve. We offer vast experience, a collection of tools, guiding questions, and resources to get started. Our Cultural Proficiency Leadership Rubric was carefully designed to guide you in your equity work, one step at a time. The following section is an opportunity to reflect on your next steps to increase your *knowledge, skills, and will* as a culturally proficient leader.

REFLECTION: KNOWLEDGE

* What steps do you need to take to raise your knowledge base and that of the key members in your community who will accompany you on this journey? What resources do you need for this?

_____

_____

_____

_____

REFLECTION: SKILLS

....

- What skills do you and those you work with currently have that will aid you in your quest for equitable education? Which skills do you need to develop in yourself and others to facilitate this journey? What resources do you need for this?

_____

_____

_____

_____

REFLECTION: WILL

....

- How will you create a sense of urgency in yourself and others to do this work? How will you raise their level of concern and caring for doing this work? How will you provide support and care for those doing this work and motivation to help them stay the course? What resources will you need for this?

_____

_____

_____

_____

The formula for success is straightforward: first adopt a moral position that all children and youth have the capacity to learn at high levels, and then create teams and networks of advocates with whom you can share your collective knowledge, skills, and will to educate *all* children. Remember that culturally proficient leaders draw on the expertise and wisdom of colleagues and the very communities they serve as a laboratory for lifelong learning in the service of others. Our work cannot be accomplished alone. The journey of achieving equity does not have an ending, but it is one we must take together.

> *"To get through the hardest journey we need take only one step at a time, but we must keep on stepping."*

—Chinese Proverb

APPENDIX

Chapter 4 Supplement

CASE STORY ONE: CARMELLA S. FRANCO

Students Denied Opportunities to Optimize Success

Analysis: Levels of the Cultural Proficiency Continuum

An analysis of this case story must acknowledge the moral imperative of the State Board of Education (SBE) to intervene in this district, where it was clear that one or more student groups were not being educated according to their needs. In such a situation, the SBE appoints a state-appointed trustee (SAT), who builds the capacity of a local district to increase student achievement. The SAT begins the process of engaging stakeholders, including local community members, to help the district align its goals to increase student outcomes. The previous inability of the district to reverse such underperformance for so long, even though data revealed persistent lack of progress, would locate the existing policies and practices of this district at either *cultural destructiveness* or *cultural incapacity*. Since data cannot reveal the intention of stakeholders to create or maintain such gaps in education for some student groups, one might assume good intentions on the part of stakeholders but conclude they were ignorant of or unskilled at implementing practices to better meet student needs. Intentionally aiming to harm a group of students by mis-educating them or minimally educating them would be considered *culturally destructive*. Absent such intentions, but still displaying ignorance of how to intervene to reverse the underperformance, the district's practice would be located at *cultural incapacity*.

The move to appoint an SAT who was compassionate, diligent, and skilled at understanding and stemming long-term systemic inequity, as well as the policies and practices of that SAT to implement targeted improvement efforts and manage the diverse perspectives of staff and the community, would align with *cultural precompetence, cultural competence,* and *Cultural Proficiency.*

Assessing Cultural Knowledge

The leader *assessed cultural knowledge* (hers and others'). She knew who some students were and learned about other cultures and perspectives among students, staff, and the community. She used data to assess that many students were not having their cultural or linguistic learning needs met. By knowing who the underserved students were and what they lacked, she was able to identify programs with a track record for meeting the needs of her students most in need. In spite of the controversy and disagreement over instructional approaches, the leader held herself and her staff accountable for the approach she believed would meet *these students'* specific needs, not those of the teachers. She understood the importance of using data to drive and justify her decisions.

Valuing Diversity

The leader *valued the diversity* of the community. It is likely that this leader was selected because of a cultural fit with the community and the need for someone with whom the community could identify and whom they could respect when difficult decisions about change were made. This leader also had to work at getting various factions of the community to value each other. Even among a particular ethnic group, there is much variety and difference in perspectives and experiences. This leader used her position to help stake-holders better know and understand each other to more effectively serve the common goal of improving student learning. Naming and claiming one's cultural identity and communicating one's pride in one's struggles and accomplishments is conducive to getting others to also stand up for themselves and have pride in who they are and what they have accomplished and can accomplish. This leader served as such a role model.

Managing the Dynamics of Difference

This leader *managed the dynamics of difference* by expecting conflict from different factions of the administration, staff, community, and even elected officials. She anticipated it and knew that trying to settle the conflict would only exacerbate the situation related to people's political beliefs and would detract from the real work at hand. She did not let the conflict derail her, and she did not try to end the conflict. Her *moral imperative* to do what was best for those students strengthened her resolve to push further in spite of the assaults coming her way. She made decisions that were unpopular with dominant voices in the school community, but did so proudly and without hesitation or apology. She used data to justify her implementation efforts and stay the course in spite of the criticism. Data are data. They tell the truth and justify the action of the leader to make controversial decisions. Data use helps *manage the dynamics of difference*. This leader took tremendous risks, personally and professionally, to carry out her plan of action to right a wrong, thereby acting in a *culturally competent* and *culturally proficient* manner. The leader also had support from a few strategic individuals at the top who she knew were backing her actions in spite of the criticism and campaigns against her. Whether she garnered this support herself or it was simply the result of confidence in her capacity, strategic support from high places is essential for leaders who go in to do the heavy lifting in situations with potential controversy, criticism, and sabotage. In time, because of the conflict and differences of opinions expressed openly, the leader was maybe even able to facilitate greater understanding between and among diverse constituents that was not present before. Often *managing the dynamics of difference* has to do with co-opting disagreement to lead to better understanding among diverse individuals and groups.

Adapting to Diversity

In this case story, the initial demonstration of *adapting to diversity* came from the SBE when it acknowledged this community's obligation to adapt to the needs of the majority of students in the school district. The data told the board that. The SBE then appointed the trustee to assess, facilitate, implement, and evaluate changes to improve student learning. The leader had to *name* the change and help the community and staff make the transition to what was an inevitable, orchestrated implementation for the benefit of the students. In the process, this leader was able to facilitate an understanding about the truth of the district's effectiveness in achieving equitable outcomes. By helping others understand the sources of their assumptions about who students were, what their needs were, and what they were capable and deserving of, she built capacity for transforming the organization's ability to achieve equitable outcomes for students.

Institutionalizing Cultural Knowledge

Through her persistent vision and her ability to garner the right resources and lead in a tense environment, this leader was able to create a culture of collaboration and decision-making focused on meeting the needs of underserved students and parents. Over time and by pressing on various leverage points in the system (recruiting, hiring, and promoting; assessment; teacher accountability; curriculum and instruction; professional development; parent and community partnerships; resource development and allocation) to change practices that could be more equitable for students, this leader might have been able to *institutionalize cultural knowledge* across the system. Transformation is long-term, over the long haul, but someone must start the ball rolling, and this leader, with her knowledge, skills, capacity, and mindset for closing gaps, was the right fit for this assignment.

CASE STORY TWO: MARIA G. OTT

District of Choice

Analysis: Levels of the Cultural Proficiency Continuum

Regarding the District of Choice initiative, this case story is clearly operational on the *left side* of the Cultural Proficiency Continuum. There are elements of the scenario that show how policies and practices promote the superiority of one or a few groups of students while excluding, limiting, or disempowering others. What keeps the scenario suspended between *cultural destructiveness* and *cultural incapacity* has to do with the intention of the policymakers, and whether they intended to benefit underserved students or their better-served counterparts. If they truly intended positive outcomes for underserved students and the results just happened to have negative consequences for some students, then the actions exhibit *cultural incapacity*. One can never know the true intentions behind a policy, so it is up to leaders to challenge the outcomes if there are clearly negative results for some student groups. This leader acted in a *culturally competent* manner by taking risks and persisting in the face of political inertia and other policy barriers to advocate for underserved students. It is possible that some of the implementation was perceived by the implementers or community/state leaders as serving everyone equally, which would put the policy at *cultural blindness* on the continuum, but too many negative consequences for too many underserved student groups obviates that possibility. The leader was operating at *cultural competence* and *Cultural Proficiency* by demanding and sharing multiple sources of data to clarify disproportional outcomes. She also took risks to challenge the extent to which implementers were holding themselves accountable for equitable outcomes, and identified actions that were incongruent with pedagogy for equity. She further acted in a *culturally proficient* manner by challenging others, including executives in high places, to dismantle this legal mandate that created barriers to success for some students.

Analysis: Essential Elements of Cultural Proficiency

Assessing Cultural Knowledge

Given the outcomes of the District of Choice initiative, it is not clear how much the implementers were bending to public pressure to provide options for some students to exit underperforming schools, as labeled by No Child

Left Behind, or if they wanted to help all children succeed. Resources and opportunities (transportation, meals, proximity to home) that some students had made it easier for them to attend a District of Choice, compared with students who did not have such resources or opportunities. Therefore, the implementers were not *assessing cultural knowledge,* as they did not take into consideration who the students were, what their needs were, and how to provide those services and meet the needs of *all* children. However, the sending district's leader did *assess cultural knowledge* and let it be known that students who needed more resources and more opportunities were not given equitable access to them.

Valuing Diversity

Since the sending and receiving districts were not working together to inform decisions for the good of the larger community, there was not a mechanism for input from the larger community before and during implementation. Since legislators representing the receiving district did not understand or *value* the perspective and plight of the sending district and its students, it could be determined that the District of Choice initiative did not *value the diversity* of the larger community. On the other hand, the leader did *value diversity* by promoting awareness of the imperative to meet the needs of all student groups, not just those with more resources and opportunities. She took risks to let it be known that the District of Choice policy was reinforcing meritocracy and a divide that already existed between the neighboring communities by promoting an entitled group of students over underserved ones.

Managing the Dynamics of Difference

The initiative was made unilaterally by a state committee, with little input from affected districts. Some input may have been sought by the designers or implementers, but it may have been just to comply with program regulations, as such input was not sustained throughout implementation or across communities. Since the initiative was a state initiative, leaders and community members may have felt intimidated to challenge the policy intentions or outcomes, or even to voice their concerns. Leaders in the sending district collected data to show the negative results of the implementation, but the data were ignored, and the sending district leaders had to take further legal action for their perspectives to be considered. It is not clear to what extent the legal challenges from the sending district affected policy requirements in other districts, beyond this one case. So in spite of the leader's bold attempts to make other perspectives known (*managing the dynamics of difference*), there was no mechanism in place to share perspectives that could have reshaped the policy. The leader attempted to *manage the dynamics of difference,* but by challenging the policy without other voices to advocate along with her, she risked creating a bigger divide in the community. However, it was clear that the leader often had to exhibit more activism than advocacy, and she accepted responsibility for being known as an activist across the state. The lesson here is that though such a stance is often necessary from an ethical perspective, it can take an emotional toll on the leader. Still, she persisted.

Adapting to Diversity

The sending district's leader acted in a *culturally competent* manner by sharing multiple sources of data that clarified patterns of disproportionality. She did that to tell the truth about the effectiveness of the policy and its negative consequences on students in her district. These data could have led to the two districts coming together to *adapt to diversity* that would serve both districts well, instead of just one. Collecting and sharing data is one way to clarify what is really going on behind a policy or practice, and collecting and sharing data is the only way to justify ongoing implementation, making changes, and holding leaders and other staff accountable for equitable outcomes. It seems that the agency that developed and implemented the District of Choice initiative did not intend to adapt to needed changes during implementation, as no data collecting or sharing mechanism was included in the implementation guidelines. This was left up to the sending district leader, but collecting data and tracking outcomes should be part of any policy implementation requirements, especially if issues of equity are a concern.

Institutionalizing Cultural Knowledge

This case story almost suggests that District of Choice policymakers wanted to avoid open communication with all stakeholder groups. It also appears that closing equity gaps was not a concern of this initiative. Rather, the intention was to reinforce a situation whereby students who had more resources and opportunities could exit an "underperforming" school or district to attend a school or district that was determined to better meet students' needs. To her credit, and acting in a *culturally proficient* manner, the sending district's leader used her position to try to influence state resources to level the playing field that had been "unleveled" by this policy. She successfully made some changes to stem the damage created in the sending district but was ultimately unable to make wholesale changes to stop the policy altogether. One might hope that if programs or schools are not meeting the needs of some or all students in a particular community, providing resources and opportunities to improve conditions at the sending schools would be a better option than raiding the pool of students already served well for an opportunity to gain access to even more resources, while leaving behind students who need additional resources.

A Cultural Proficiency mindset requires that we not label students (or schools) as "underperforming" but as "underserved" so the blame and responsibility for improvement shifts from the students (or their parents) to the adults in the system who must learn how to better meet the needs of students, especially those most underserved in the past. The entire notion of the District of Choice initiative seems conceived from the standpoint of blame for the students and schools, labeled by some external criteria as "underperforming," and is *culturally destructive* to the students and communities that public education serves. If blaming our clients for their lack of resources and opportunities for success in school is the paradigm of educational leaders and policymakers, then closing education or societal gaps will never come to pass, and we can never hope to institutionalize equitable change for schools or society.

CASE STORY THREE: DARLINE P. ROBLES

Importance of Data and Informed Decision-Making

Analysis: Levels of the Cultural Proficiency Continuum

This is a very rich and complex situation to analyze, and most likely, this analysis will not be comprehensive. First, one must consider the consciousness of the executive decision-makers in this large public school system to see the writing on the wall about concerns that would inevitably be asserted by underserved constituents. Their anticipation of the future, followed by their outreach and hiring of *this* specific superintendent, who had experience in collaborative decision-making with diverse communities and creating equity-driven systems, was nothing less than a *culturally proficient* decision, especially since it took some degree of humility and risk to recognize their own incapacity and to surrender to someone they thought knew how to do what they could not. Beyond that decision, there appeared to be many practices operating at *cultural incapacity* and *cultural blindness* in the district prior to the new superintendent. Absent any conscious displays of causing intentional harm to some students, there were still some policies and procedures that effectively maintained the status quo by benefiting those who reflected attributes of the dominant culture, while limiting improvements for underserved community members and students. This demonstrated *cultural incapacity.* Some evidence that the district believed a culture of improvement for all students, regardless of their cultural backgrounds, was good enough for everyone suggests *cultural blindness.* Prior to the new superintendent, it appears that involving members of the diverse community to participate in significant ways was most likely done to comply with agency requirements but not necessarily to learn how to better serve those members of the community (*cultural blindness* and *cultural precompetence*). Whether or not leaders were intimidated by how to solicit or how to include multiple voices, the fact remains that certain communities' needs remained unrepresented; so little or no movement was made to find out what was needed to close educational gaps for them. This shows how even neutral intentions have negative consequences (*cultural incapacity*). Kudos to the district for making a strategic intervention in how it handled business by hiring the new superintendent before inflection points would have demanded such. The district "got it" but didn't necessarily know what to do about it; so they hired a partner who could and would build knowledge and capacity (*cultural precompetence*).

The new superintendent was obviously experienced, seasoned, and bold, with a track record for doing the work the district knew they needed but did not know how to do. The district hired a leader who was Latina and was also a highly educated, competent, experienced, and successful professional. These intersecting aspects of who she was changed the larger assumption among staff and leaders in the district that one could not be all those things at the same time. Even a *culturally precompetent* perspective such as this, with no malice intended, leads to decisions that serve some students better than others by not holding high expectations for them.

By simply being who she was, the new leader challenged assumptions about her identity, resulting in cognitive dissonance for many. Not wanting to make any "bold" moves beyond "who she was" at the onset, the leader may have kept a low profile at first, not making any drastic changes to policies or practices until she garnered support from less-heard-from communities and business leaders. Once armed with new thoughts and perspectives that were not hers alone, she had support to start examining data in more robust ways than had been done in the past. She used multiple data sources and then disaggregated and cross-tabulated longitudinal data so district constituents could know the truth about how well some students were or were not being served up to that point. Data are the best way to get constituents on board in non-polarizing, non-contentious, no-blame ways. This was a game changer for a district that thought it was doing the best it could by simply being a district of continuous improvement. Public figures and the press love improvement data—it looks like everyone is winning. But in spite of the positive political optics, improvement data often hide the dirty little secrets of racial disproportionality. Collecting and sharing data in this way, this leader facilitated an understanding about the district's status quo across the educational community and laid the groundwork for understanding underperformance linked to underutilization of resources, thereby shifting deficit thinking about diverse stakeholders. Hence, she managed the dynamics of difference at a level of *Cultural Proficiency*.

Even though this leader was in this district for only eight years, she knew that to *institutionalize cultural knowledge* across the system after she departed, she would have to change the mindset. She was aiming not just for change but for a kind of deeper transformation that changes people's thinking in profound ways. No amount of new decisions, revised policies, and structures can paradigmatically change the way people see and do things. Anticipating a day in the future when she might not be the one taking the lead, and wanting to build capacity for the work, this leader invested resources in Cultural Proficiency training. She held high expectations across the system for everyone to participate. By so doing, she facilitated an understanding that meeting the needs of all students, especially those most underserved in the past, contributed to the common good. That moral imperative, reinforced by training and relentless data analysis and discussions, positioned this district to continue raising its knowledge base while building capacity for the future. Eventually, for transformation to occur, the driving force needs to come from inside the system itself, regardless of who the leader is. Often developing leadership in others is more important than being a leader oneself. While creating a legacy for herself was probably the last thing on her mind, it seems probable that this leader did leave a legacy—one of advocacy and bold action to accomplish what others before her had not been able to do. Her approach changed people in profound personal ways so their lens for educating students would benefit not only current students but students to come. On the Cultural Proficiency Continuum, there is a point where we are conscious about our ignorance. This "aha moment" shifts our examination from who *others are* and *what they can and cannot do* to who *we are* and *what we can and must do*. Then, for a few leaders, there is a stage beyond the aha, where the leader is no longer seeking to learn how to *become* culturally proficient, but says and does things that show a profound understanding of themselves and others and what is the best course to follow for equitable schools and a just society. This is the ideal orbit for the culturally proficient leader. They simply *are*!

SAMPLE CASE STORY FOR APPLICATION

How One Superintendent Used Data to Drive Change

Analysis: Essential Elements of Cultural Proficiency

Assessing Cultural Knowledge

The leader was a compassionate, diligent, and transformational professional whose life experiences led to a profound understanding of long-term systemic educational inequity. She had culturally specific professional experience that compelled a relentless, fervent professional and personal commitment to challenge and break down barriers to educational opportunities and success while closing gaps for historically underserved stakeholders. The leader proudly asserted her own culture while nurturing relationships and amplifying voices and perspectives that had been previously discouraged or ignored. The leader perceived her own and others' cultural assets as strengths and held herself and others accountable for learning about and meeting the needs of underserved students, not the needs of those with the loudest voices or most dominant presence.

Valuing Diversity

This leader *valued diversity*: she embraced it and taught other people to see it and value it as well. By modeling a positive cultural identity, she may have helped others develop positive cultural identities about themselves and value, respect, and seek out the diversity in the district, including the diversity of opinions and perspectives. The leader considered the cultural backgrounds of others when recruiting and hiring, and promoted diverse representation among school committees, staff, and administrators. She understood the influence of culture on learning and teaching, and promoted culture as an asset for adult performance and student success.

Managing the Dynamics of Difference

Because the leader intended to "confront the ugly truth" about the district's effectiveness in meeting all students' needs, she anticipated disagreement and conflict. Rather than stemming the conflict, she harnessed it to illuminate common understanding about "the elephant in the room" and gather diverse perspectives about the status quo and what to do about it.

The leader encouraged diverse opinions and shared them across cultures and the district in non-contentious and non-polarizing ways. Such sharing helped the organization learn about and prioritize student needs and promote organizational flexibility to meet them. She embraced risk-taking and made decisions, which may not have been popular with the dominant cultures or decision-makers. Nevertheless, she persisted in the face of criticism and took personal responsibility for any professional consequences of her advocacy for underserved students and silent stakeholders.

Adapting to Diversity

The leader understood the importance of data and using data in multiple ways to create a collective understanding and responsibility for identifying and meeting the needs of underserved students. She built an understanding that improvement was not the goal; closing gaps was! She accelerated data understanding by moving beyond an examination of just achievement data to also include access and opportunity data. Students cannot achieve if they do not have access to quality resources and opportunities to learn.

Institutionalizing Cultural Knowledge

The leader was not afraid to make others aware of equity gaps and the ineffectiveness of the system to meet current students' needs. Neither was she afraid to make decisions that primarily supported underserved students. She used her position to educate everyone within and even outside the organization about the district's failures and its changing paradigm for embracing equity over equality and closing gaps over continuous improvement. To institutionalize change, she invested in Cultural Proficiency training to encourage a moral imperative and equity pedagogy in all departments across the system, and in the community as well, and to build appropriate knowledge, skills, and attitude for maintaining an equity-driven system for the present and to influence the future.

REFERENCES

Cross, T. L., Bazron, B. J., Dennis, K. W., & Isaacs, M. R. (1989). *Toward a culturally competent system of care* (Vol. 1). Georgetown University Child Development Program, Child and Adolescent Service System Program.

Daramola, E. J. (2021, October). *Centering the family in the family liaison role.* School of Education, University of Southern California.

Escalante, J. (1990). Jaime Escalante's math program. *Journal of Negro Education, 59*(3), 407–423.

Franco, C. S., Ott, M. G., & Robles, D. P. (2011). *A culturally proficient society begins in school: Leadership for equity.* Corwin.

Frankenberg, E., Ee, J., Ayscue, J. B., & Orfield, G. (2019, May 10). *Harming our common future: America's segregated schools 65 years after* Brown. The Civil Rights Project and Center for Education and Civil Rights. https://www.civilrightsproject.ucla.edu/research/k-12-education/integration-and-diversity/harming-our-common-future-americas-segregated-schools-65-years-after-brown/Brown-65-050919v4-final.pdf

Fullan, M. (2003). *The moral imperative of school leadership.* Corwin.

Gentry, M., & Fugate, C. M. (2012, June 14). Gifted Native American students: Underperforming, under-identified, and overlooked. *Psychology in Schools, 49*(7), 631–646. https://doi.org/10.1002/pits.21624

Hemingway, E. (1999). *A farewell to arms.* Vintage Classics.

Hilliard, A. G., III. (1991, September). Do we have the will to educate all children? *Educational Leadership, 49*(1), 31–36.

Hotchkiss, M. (2016, July 20). Economics, culture intersect to shape Asian Americans' academic advantage. *Princeton University.* https://www.princeton.edu/news/2016/07/20/economics-culture-intersect-shape-asian-americans-academic-advantage

Howard, T. C. (2020, June 21). Statements supporting Black Lives Matter are not enough. Schools must demand more. *EdSource.* https://edsource.org/2020/statements-supporting-black-lives-matter-are-not-enough-schools-must-do-more/633978

Huerta, D. (2016, October 27). Election day is the most important day of your life. *HuffPost.* https://www.huffpost.com/entry/election-day-is-the-most-important-day-of-your-life_b_5810eb7de4b06e45c5c70185

Kendi, I. X. (2019). *How to be an antiracist.* One World.

Lewis, J. (2018, June 27). *Do not get lost in a sea of despair. Be hopeful, be optimistic. Our struggle is not the struggle of a day* [Tweet]. Twitter. https://twitter.com/repjohnlewis/

status/1011991303599607808? s=20&
t=0A7kR6dAnCuGUDZw0NZG9A

Lindsey, R. B., Nuri-Robins, K., & Terrell, R. D. (2009). *Cultural proficiency: A manual for school leaders* (3rd ed.). Corwin.

Lindsey, R. B., Roberts, L. M., & Campbell Jones, F. (2013). *The culturally proficient school: An implementation guide for school leaders* (2nd ed.). Corwin.

Liu, A., & Xie, Y. (2016, July). Why do Asian Americans academically outperform whites? The cultural explanation revisited. *Social Science Research, 58,* 210–216. https://doi.org/10.1016/j.ssresearch.2016.03.004

Nellum, C. (2021). *Newsletter.* Education Trust-West.

Nuri-Robins, K., Lindsey, D. B., Lindsey, R. B., & Terrel, R. D. (2011). *Culturally proficient instruction: A guide for people who teach* (3rd ed.). Corwin.

Perie, M., Moran, R., & Lutkus, A. D. (2005). *NAEP 2004 trends in academic progress: Three decades of student performance in reading and mathematics* (NCES 2005–464). U.S. Department of Education, Institute of Education Sciences, National Center for Education Statistics.

Reardon, S. (2014, September 1). Income inequality affects our children's educational opportunities. In H. Bouchey & E. Paisley (Eds.), *Building a strong foundation for the U.S. economy: Understanding whether and how economic inequality affects economic growth* (pp. 26–28). Washington Center for Equitable Growth. https://equitablegrowth.org/income-inequality-affects-our-childrens-educational-opportunities/

Rueda, R. (2011). *The three dimensions of improving student performance: Finding the right solutions to the right problems.* Teachers College Press.

Saavedra, A. R., & Polikoff, M. (2021, June 13). Analysis: Tutoring, summer school, pods—Survey finds parents aren't so thrilled about most K–12 COVID recovery solutions on the table. *The 74.* https://www.the74million.org/article/analysis-tutoring-summer-school-pods-survey-finds-parents-arent-so-thrilled-about-most-k-12-covid-recovery-solutions-on-the-table/

Shaw, K. (Director). (2022). *Let the little light shine* [Documentary]. ITVS International.

Yeakley, A., & Brett, T. (2020, September 16). *Tips and techniques for facilitating dialogues online* [virtual workshop].

Yoon, S. Y., & Gentry, M. (2009). Racial and ethnic representation in gifted programs: Current status of and implications for gifted Asian American students. *Gifted Child Quarterly, 53*(2), 121–136. https://doi.org/10.1177/0016986208330564

Zuñiga, X., Nagda, B. A., Chesler, M., & Cytron-Walker, A. (2007). Intergroup dialogue in higher education: Meaningful learning about social justice. *ASHE Higher Education Report, 32*(4), 1–128.

Zúñiga, X., Nagda, B. A., & Sevig, T. D. (2002). Intergroup dialogues: An educational model for cultivating engagement across differences. *Equity and Excellence in Education, 35*(1), 7–17.

INDEX

Mindsets, 9–10, 19, 41, 58
  for equity, 19, 58
Motivation, 28–29, 83–84, 86, 103
Movement, 17, 26, 92

Native American students, 77
NCLB (No Child Left Behind), 57, 96
Nellum, C., 94

Online learning, 2, 18, 25, 95
Oppression, 5, 9, 93

Pandemic, 1–2, 18, 25
Passion, 28–29, 98, 101–2
Pedagogy, 13, 34, 36, 84
Polikoff, M. S., 95
Poverty, 9, 50, 53, 71, 82
Power, 36, 42–43, 86
Principals, 49, 63–64, 66, 74, 82, 96
  school-site, 58
Principles, 3, 16, 22–23, 100
  guiding, 3, 11, 13, 16–17,
    22–23, 100
Professional development, 19–20, 74
Programs, 19, 29, 31, 33–34, 43,
    48, 65, 77, 95
  changes, 16
  first intergroup dialogue, 99
  leaders support, 29

Racial/ethnic groups, 3, 14, 56, 70,
    71, 73, 76–78, 84, 94, 92–95.
    See also AAPI, African Americans,
    Asian Americans, Children of color,
    Filipino, Latinx
Racism, 1, 5, 9, 93–94
Readiness, 16, 19, 37, 69, 89
Reardon, S., 75
Resistance, 10, 12, 94, 97
Responsibilities, 6, 8, 32, 34, 51, 84
Risks, 2, 26, 32, 36, 42, 46, 54–55,
    61–62, 77, 84–85
  taking, 32, 42, 46, 54, 61
Romer, R., 47
Rubrics, 20, 26–27, 38–39

Saavedra, A. R., 95
SBE (State Board of Education), 42, 44
School districts, 14, 25, 42, 48,
    52, 56–57, 76
  medium-sized, 46
  neighboring, 50
  new, 55
  takeover, 4
  traditional, 100
  urban, 1, 55
School systems, 4, 8, 11, 15, 72, 83, 89, 96
  equitable, 80
Sexual orientation, 14
Shaw, K., 86
Social justice, 26–27, 32, 34, 92–93, 99
  work, 101
Socioeconomic status, 70, 76–78, 84
Southern California Rossier School, 4
Stakeholders, 12–13, 16, 23, 28–33,
    35–36, 70, 72, 77, 79–81, 83,
    85–86, 89, 97–98
  diverse, 31
  external, 86–88
  groups, 31, 35–36, 100
  key, 81, 100
  underserved, 28–29, 33–36
  use of input, 70, 85
Standards, dominant culture's, 36
State Board of Education (SBE), 42, 44
Superintendents, 4, 8, 46, 52, 55, 58, 63,
    65–67, 83
Systemic oppression, 11–12, 16
  historical, 93

Teams, 64, 81–82, 85, 88,
    101, 104
Tension, 11, 16
Tenure, 4, 44, 55, 58–60
Textbooks, 14, 16–17, 19
Training, 4–5, 74, 89
Transient students, 64–65
Transportation, home-to-school, 48, 51
Truth, 13, 33, 59–60, 72, 83, 96

U.S. Census Bureau, 79, 80

A SAGE Publishing Company

Helping educators make the greatest impact

CORWIN HAS ONE MISSION: to enhance education through intentional professional learning.

We build long-term relationships with our authors, educators, clients, and associations who partner with us to develop and continuously improve the best evidence-based practices that establish and support lifelong learning.